DATE DUE

AUG 2 2 1998	
NOV 1 0 1998	
NOV 2 4 2001	
SEP 1 3 2004	

GAYLORD   PRINTED IN U.S.A.

Echoes of the Ancient World

Series editor Werner Forman

BYZANTIUM

BYZANTIUM
City of Gold, City of Faith

Text by Paul Hetherington

Photographs by Werner Forman

ORBIS PUBLISHING · LONDON

For Virginia, Andrew and Francesca

Half-title page:
Byzantine gold cup with personifications, or tyches of the cities of Roms, Constantinople, Alexandria
and Cyprus — c. sixth century. The side shown here is Constantinople.

Title-page:
Byzantine artists depicted saintly subjects in deep reds, blues and greens against an unearthly luminescence
of gold. Thus in the vast but barely visible space of their churches, candlelight produced extraordinary effects.
A single dim light reflects down the entire length of this fourteenth-century vault. St Mark's, Venice.

Letter B from an eleventh- or twelfth-century illuminated manuscript, Athens, codex 2363, folio 263.r.

This page:
Detail from Missorium of Theodosius — Theodosius enthroned.

© 1983 Orbis Publishing Limited, London
First published in Italy by Istituto Geografico De Agostini,
S.p.A., Novara, 1981

Printed in Czechoslovakia
ISBN-0-85613-363-9
50150

CONTENTS

Above: Initial T from illuminated manuscript. Eleventh or twelfth century. Athens, codex 2363, folio 3. v.

Left: Although probably dating from between the ninth and eleventh centuries, this area of cut and inlaid marble would have been laid on the floor of a Byzantine palace in conscious emulation of similar ancient Roman work. This type of mosaic is known as opus sectile, or 'cut work', and involved a much higher degree of skill to execute than conventional mosaic. The Romans expended much ingenuity on illusionistic patterns such as this.

THE BYZANTINES

The Byzantines took their name from the small Greek colony founded during the seventh century BC on the shores of the Bosporos. Tradition has it that the founder of this colony was called Byzas, and he called his town Byzantium. The Bosporos is the narrow channel which both links the Aegean with the Black Sea and divides Europe from Asia, and so it was always of great strategic importance. The modern visitor to this site will find himself in the teeming modern city of Istanbul, but this is actually its third name. 'Istanbul' means 'into the City' and this was the word the Turks used to refer to it after they had captured the city in 1453. For most of its history the city was known as Constantinople, in honour of the Roman Emperor Constantine, who founded his new capital on the site of Byzantium early in the fourth century AD.

It is not possible to give very precise limits to the period of the existence of many civilizations of the past, but it can be said with complete certainty that the Byzantine Empire lasted for 1123 years and eighteen days. This was the huge lapse of time between the inauguration of the new city by Constantine on 11 May 330, and the day of the final assault on its battered walls by the Turkish troops of Sultan Mehmet, that took place on 29 May 1453.

Who were the Byzantines? To answer this question, it is necessary to take a brief look at the Roman world at the time that Constantine first came to power in 306. The vast Roman Empire, stretching from the north of England to Mesopotamia, was at the time deeply divided by civil war, and its economy was racked by savage inflation; great areas of productive land were depopulated, and all the measures that the emperors took to improve matters were useless. These chaotic conditions were aggravated by two other important factors. One was the cosmopolitan character of the Empire: one of the great achievements of the Romans had been to create a society to which the concept of nationality was in effect unknown — every free man was a citizen of the Empire. While the Empire lasted this was a noble ideal, but as it began to disintegrate this unifying force was lost as well. The other very clear characteristic of the Roman world at this time was the welter of religions that flourished there. As the confusion of the Empire increased, so the number of its religions multiplied and diversified.

The last major bout of persecution of Christians, lasting about two years, had just ended in 305. The cause of this final outbreak is interesting for the light it sheds on the troubled minds of the world leaders at that time. Just a few years before, the Emperor Diocletian had been sacrificing to obtain omens for his next military campaign. When his soothsayers examined the victims' livers they said they could not see any of the usual signs. Further

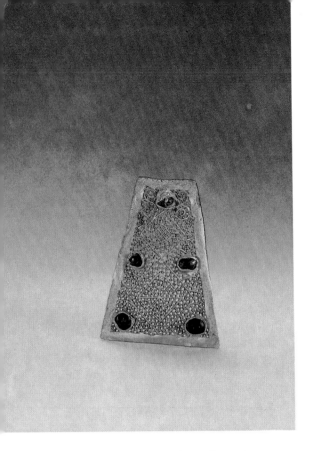

This small fragment of jewellery would have been fastened, with others, to cloth or leather to form a necklace. Dating as it does from the fourth century, its very fine openwork decoration contains an early use of the XP symbol, which provides the first two letters of the Greek form of Christ's name. The stones are garnets, and the piece indicates the high artistic standards available in Constantinople from the earliest decades.

animals were sacrificed, but again favourable signs were absent. The chief soothsayer, Tagis, eventually said that the sacrifices were not working because there were profane people in attendance. He was referring to some Christian officials who had been making the sign of the cross during the pagan sacrifice. The Emperor Diocletian, in great anger, ordered that not only all members of his court, but all civil servants and the entire Roman Army should sacrifice to the pagan gods or be dismissed. The anti-Christian feeling among the Roman leadership was expressed with most zeal by Diocletian's Caesar, Galerius, who did all he could to have church buildings destroyed, all copies of the scriptures surrendered and burnt, and to make everyone sacrifice to the pagan gods. Resistance was frequently met by death. This policy was pursued, particularly in the Eastern Mediterranean, for about two years. Then political problems, combined with the illness and abdication of Diocletian in 305, forced its abandonment. It was against this background of religious intolerance and strife, combined with great political and financial insecurity, that Constantine was raised to imperial power in York, in 306. As Constantine rapidly came to wield the absolute power of sole emperor, he must have realized that a fundamentally new approach to religious problems was needed. He took two measures for which he will be remembered throughout world history. First, in a pronouncement known as the Edict of Milan he established that the followers of all religions, but specifically Christians, were to be given freedom of worship. Second — and perhaps even more important — he decided to create a completely new capital, which would leave behind in Western Europe all the chaotic burden of the past. This new capital, founded on the site of Byzantium, was to be called Constantinople.

So the Byzantines were the people who came from all over the known world to inhabit the new city. They were in fact a tremendously varied mixture of peoples. There would have been many new settlers from the Greek islands and mainland, as well as from areas to the north — Macedonia, Thrace and Dacia; the provinces of Asia Minor, such as Bithynia and Armenia, would also have provided much of the new population. Syrians and Arabians, as well as Egyptians, would have been present. And there would certainly have been high-ranking officials attracted from Italy by the inducements of palaces of which the tenure was linked to income from estates in Asia Minor.

It might seem strange that, in searching for a solution to the problems of the divided and strife-ridden Empire that he had inherited, Constantine should assemble such a diverse population. There were, however, three elements which provided a dynamically unifying force. The first of these was language: Latin had always been the universal language of the Empire, and there would have been no question of any other form of communication being adopted — it was the only living and proven international language. The second was provided by the nature of Constantine's new foundation. It was not just any new frontier town, given the name of its founder. It was to be the new capital of the Roman Empire — 'New Rome', as it was at once called. Its inhabitants were intensely proud of this cultural ancestry, and to the bitter end insisted on being called Romans — *Romaioi*. Also, as part of this Roman heritage, the Byzantines from the start adopted a framework of Roman administration and law; it was therefore on well-tried Roman principles that the new government was installed. The third factor, which was of utmost importance, was that Constantinople was from the start a Christian city — the first such foundation in history. Constantine never allowed pagan rites to be celebrated in the city, and although there were one or two pagan temples there before his adoption of the site, they were never subsequently used. He had a number of churches built there as

Right: Throughout the ancient world it was customary to mark bread with stamps such as this. Here, the name ΛΕΟΝΤΙΟΥ implies that he is the owner of the stamp and baker of the bread. The seven-branched candlestick, originally a Jewish symbol, was taken over by the Christians of the third and fourth century, and reinterpreted to mean 'Christ, the Light of the World'. This stamp could therefore have been intended for either Jewish or Christian use.

Below: This scene from the base of the obelisk which the Emperor Theodosius erected in the Hippodrome in Constantinople shows Persians and Dacians bringing tribute to the Emperor. Both groups can be distinguished by their characteristic clothing and headgear. It is from works of sculpture such as this that an idea can be gained of the wide variety of ethnic types which made up the population of the city in the fourth and fifth centuries.

part of his grandiose overall plan for the city, as well as having many copies of the scriptures specially made and imported at his expense for the use of the new population.

The features of Constantine's foundation of the city that suggest that he intended a complete break with the past mainly centre round his attitude to religion. His conversion to Christianity had certainly taken place in 312, although the precise nature of his conversion — whether it was mainly political, or the result of genuine religious conviction — is still debated. The only first-hand record of his motives in founding this new city that is known is his own affirmation that he acted 'on God's command'. Yet he was only baptized shortly before his death, and it is possible to find evidence of some ambivalence in Constantine's attitude to his new city. While he raised its status far above that of the usual provincial city foundation, he

did not in fact grant it the full political framework of a capital. It was for instance only placed under the governorship of a proconsul, not that of a city prefect. It was provided with a senate, but its members were only entitled to be called *clari* (distinguished), not *clarissimi* (most distinguished), as were those of ancient Rome. Its inhabitants only received free rations of bread, while those of Rome also enjoyed, as of right, distributions of beef, pork and wine as well.

This ambivalence, which is not to be found in the later traditions concerning the founding of the city, is quite easily explained if it is realized in what overwhelmingly high regard the ancient capital of the Roman Empire was held. Although Constantine was himself a native of Naissus (the modern Niš) in Serbia, he must always have regarded Rome as the historic and sentimental capital of the Empire — and indeed of the world. To found a new capital in direct opposition, as it were, to ancient Rome, must have appeared to be almost a form of sacrilege. Rome was the place, for example, where Constantine's mother, Helena, was buried (in about

Porphyry, of which this group of four figures in St Mark's, Venice is made, was a kind of marble reserved only for imperial use. As there was a short period early in the fourth century when there were four emperors ruling simultaneously over the vast but disintegrating Roman Empire, it is usually thought that this group of embracing emperors represents the intended harmony of their rule.

330), and his daughter as well (in about 350). It was only some time later, when the western parts of the Empire were decimated by Goths and Vandals, that the foundation of Constantinople began to take on the character of a completely revolutionary action.

The Byzantines can be defined simply as the inhabitants of Constantinople during the millenium and more of its existence. While their outward characteristics were always changing, they never lost the sense of their ultimately Roman origins.

Initially, the motives which moved the new population to arrive and fill the city must have been very mixed. In an unstable world, the chance for a fresh start must have had considerable attraction. The knowledge that the official policy of a major new leader was to encourage in every way the success of his new capital would certainly have held the promise of financial rewards; this must have motivated many of those who moved there. It is unlikely that the vision of the new capital as a centre for the new religion would have figured very largely in the first decades of its existence, although this must have been the inspiration for some. And as the centuries passed, and the city stood alone as a stronghold of Christianity in the Eastern Mediterranean, this religious ardour would come to be shared by all the population. There would always be a constant strain of Greek blood among the Byzantines, but this was persistently being amalgamated with other ethnic types — Asiatics, Scythians, Egyptians and Slavs. Even the Byzantine emperors were of very mixed blood: Arcadius, for example, was of Spanish descent, and married to a Goth, Eudoxia, while the main dynasty of the seventh century was of Arabic extraction. Their language, too, underwent great changes. The pure Latin of Constantine's age was soon giving way to Greek, and by the seventh century this had become the *lingua franca* of the Capital. Byzantine culture therefore relied for its extraordinary unity on ideals rather than on any external or imposed uniformity: the ideal of a noble Roman past, and the ideal of an orthodox, mystic Christian faith.

The serene harmony of this fourth-century relief exemplifies the confident world view of the early Christians. The empty throne awaits the Second Coming of Christ, while two lambs, symbolic of the apostles, suggest the imminence of Paradise.

CONSTANTINOPLE DURING THE EARLY CENTURIES

Above: Constantine, the founder of New Rome, is portrayed here on a gold solidus minted at Nicomedia in 335. The artist who cut the die for this coin clearly intended the first Christian Emperor to be seen looking upwards 'as though speaking with God', as it was expressed by his biographer, Eusebius.

Left: The importation and erection of an Egyptian obelisk in the hippodrome at Constantinople by Emperor Theodosius would have been regarded as a link with the practices of Ancient Rome. This detail from the base, which he had made, shows the Emperor seated between his two sons. Their identical position conveys the formality of court life that was being established, while the slight differentiation in scale, with the more important individual shown larger, is an aristic convention that was to be much developed later.

What was the layout of the city as Constantine would have known it? Any new foundation of his age would have had to be furnished with a substantial range of public buildings. Besides an administrative centre, these would have included a planned road system linking the main areas of the city, baths, forums, a hippodrome or circus for races, probably a theatre, provision for water storage, places of worship and a palace for the ruler. Some of these already existed on the site of Byzantium before Constantine adopted it as his new capital; there was a hippodrome there, which he enlarged, and some grandiose public baths. But for the most part he supervised the construction of a completely new city — a city, furthermore, which was to be the entirely new capital of the only universal empire that the world had then known.

Among the buildings that Constantine provided, besides the hippodrome and baths, were a number of minor palaces as well as a Great Palace for himself, a large forum, a building for the Senate, a large open courtyard called the Augusteion in memory of his mother, Helena Augusta, three large churches and a number of smaller ones. These were linked by a major road called the Mese, or 'middle road'. Also, and of great importance, he had built a major system of fortified walls. One of the great natural features of the site of Constantinople — indeed it must have been an influential factor in the choice of location — was a superb natural harbour; this was known from earliest times as The Horn, and later as The Golden Horn. This also had to be included in the defences.

All the early descriptions of Constantinople stress the large numbers of sculptures with which Contantine endowed his new capital. These were gathered from all over the Mediterranean, and relatively few were the work of contemporary sculptors. There were over eighty bronze statues in the Baths of Zeuxippus (the major public baths) alone; more statues lined the Mese, peopled the squares and main buildings; watching over the deliberations of the Senate was a figure of Zeus from Dodona, one of Pallas from Lindos, and a group of the muses from Helicon. St Jerome even commented disapprovingly that Constantinople was 'endowed with the nudity of every other city' (*'Dedicatur Constantinopolis omnium paene urbium nuditas'*). When speculating on the approach of Constantine to his newly adopted Christian faith, and on how he related it to the pagan past of Rome, it is interesting to remember that when he set up a statue of himself on a porphyry (purple marble) column in the main forum, he did not commission a modern work but adapted a bronze statue of Apollo that he had had brought from Phrygia. This is the sort of detail which reveals that Constantine intended his capital to be seen in most major respects as very much a 'New Rome'.

The modern visitor to Istanbul will find very little trace of the splendour of the city as it would have been on its inauguration in 330. The famous hippodrome can still be identified, but it is now just a flat, park-like space, with kiosks selling coffee and soft drinks, and the renowned 'Blue Mosque' is the nearest major building. If the visitor wants shelter from the gusty, gritty wind that seems to blow perpetually across the city, he may walk from the 'hippodrome' to the cover of the Grand Bazaar, and so traverse part of the layout of Constantine's forum and road system. He may see on his way the one chief surviving relic of the age of the founder, the famous 'Burnt Column'. By some extraordinary chance, the porphyry column set up by Constantine which originally bore the statue of the Emperor still stands. Now braced by many metal bands, it has looked down on innumerable changes in the area round it. Scorched and blackened by the flames of over sixty fires that have swept across this part of the city, it is now a sad but defiant reminder of the days of the city's early grandeur. For the rest, one can find the main modern roads still following those laid out in the initial foundation, and the sites of all Constantine's largest churches are still to be located under later structures. In spite of the reverence with which the first Christian Emperor's foundations were treated by later Byzantine rulers, the Great Palace was so dilapidated even by the thirteenth century that it could no longer be used; its ruins were adapted to become simultaneously a quiet retreat for monks, and latrines for the common people.

All three of Constantine's major church buildings have disappeared. Two — those dedicated to St Sofia ('Holy Wisdom') and St Irene ('Holy Peace') — were of basic basilica plan, and probably for that reason were never the subject of detailed descriptions. This type of building, known all over the Roman world as a place of public assembly, consisted of a long, open rectangular space, with a pitched wooden roof; down each side, and divided from the central area by columns, were one or two aisles, which had a lower roof level. The third, dedicated to the Holy Apostles (so known as the 'Apostoleion') was of much more original design. Taken in conjunction with his statue in the forum it reveals a great deal about how he regarded

Above: The sequence of reliefs on the base of the Egyptian obelisk constitutes one of the best surviving records of events and ceremonies in the hippodrome in the fourth century. In this relief on the north-west side of the base, the Emperor is seen seated between his sons, receiving tribute from subject peoples.

Right: During the centuries of Turkish rule in the city, many of the original Byzantine fortifications were changed or modernized. Examples of this can be found in the additions to the complex round the Golden Gate and the so-called 'Seven Towers Castle' seen here.

14

both himself and his new capital; he had a remarkably clear view of his reign as standing at a cross-roads of history, with the world of pagan antiquity behind him and a new, Christian world view developing before him. The Apostoleion, according to admiring contemporary descriptions, was a very large building designed on the plan of an equal-armed cross, and was from its conception intended to be the Emperor's mausoleum. At the crossing of the arms there was a high drum, pierced by windows and covered by some form of conical roof. Under this, in the very centre of the building, stood Constantine's sarcophagus surrounded by an enclosure. The sarcophagus was in porphyry — the purple marble reserved for imperial use — while the walls were clad in sheets of marble of other colours. Most interesting of all, round the sarcophagus stood twelve piers or cenotaphs representing the twelve apostles. Constantine did not just regard himself as the heir to the Caesars; he also saw himself as Christ's representative on earth, and as the thirteenth apostle.

The founder of the city was probably only fifty when he died in 337, seven years after its dedication. Had he lived even another twenty years he would have seen spectacular growth in the size of the city and its population. In the 360s a new harbour was built facing on to the Sea of Marmara, to supplement the Golden Horn. In the 370s the Emperor Valens (364—78) built a large new aqueduct to improve the water supplies of the expanding city. His successor, Theodosius (379—95), added to the central *spina* of the hippodrome (the low wall down the centre, round which the races took place), the most spectacular of monuments, a tall Egyptian obelisk made of finely carved syenite (grey granite). While the hieroglyphs on the obelisk itself date from the time of Thutmosis III (1504—1450 BC) the reliefs on the large pedestal display some of the most interesting and best-documented art of the Theodosian age. In one of them the Emperor can be seen with his family and courtiers presiding over a session of the games; he holds a wreath in readiness to place on the head of the victor. In another he is shown with Valentinian II, Arcadius and Honorius, seated in the imperial box receiving tribute from subject barbarian tribes. These reliefs give by far the best evidence available regarding the appearance and usage of this, the most important part of the hippodrome, and they show how

Although now incorporated into the great circuit of the land walls, this gateway, called the Golden Gate, was originally a free-standing triumphal arch. It was erected by Emperor Theodosius the Great, and the central archway of the triple gate originally supported a statue of the Emperor and an inscription. Even now, the whole ensemble is strongly reminiscent of the imperial Roman origins of the city.

In the small Church of SS Sergius and Bacchus, built by the Emperor Justinian almost adjoining the Great Palace, it is possible to glimpse in microcosm some of the immensely daring spatial qualities that were later to emerge on a much vaster scale in Hagia Sophia. One can also see here some of the attempts to form a new sculptural language in the carving of the capitals, for which the Emperor's sculptors were striving.

close the continuity was between this aspect of life in the new capital and life in ancient Rome.

No emperor's reign would have passed without additions being made to the public buildings of the city, or to their decoration. Further roads and forums were constantly being constructed, and private houses were being built continuously to shelter the ever-increasing population. There are no dependable figures for the early population of Constantinople, but an interesting list of all the buildings it contained can be found in the *Notitia Dignitatum*, a factual record dating from about a century after the city's foundation. By then, if this text is correct, there were, in addition to the buildings already mentioned, two theatres, 153 private baths and eight public ones, fifty-two porticoes, five granaries, eight aqueducts or water reservoirs, four large official meeting halls, fourteen churches, fourteen palaces, and 4383 large houses, as well as innumerable smaller dwellings. Even allowing for some exaggeration, the population by this time must surely have been between half a million and a million inhabitants.

A characteristic enrichment of the city was made by the Emperor Arcadius (395—408), whose life-style was notoriously luxurious and flamboyant. He had erected a column covered with narrative relief carvings of his father, Theodosius', victories over the Goths and Ostrogoths. It was in this way a clear continuation of the classical Roman columns of Trajan and Marcus Aurelius which still stand in Rome. Arcadius' column was some fifty metres (160 feet) high, and so was at least as high as that of Constantine; it was set up in a new forum and dedicated in 402. Today only the plinth remains — a typical reminder of the city's former splendour, now decayed.

It was under Theodosius II (408—50) that the largest and most decisive change was made to the appearance of Constantinople since its foundation. His reign, which virtually covered the first half of the fifth century, saw the construction of the huge system of fortifications that is still today massively impressive. This enormous project was necessary for two reasons. By the fifth century the original land walls of Constantine simply did not enclose sufficient territory, and many houses had been built outside them in unprotected open country. The other reason was more sinister. There was bad news from the West. In 410 Alaric invaded and sacked Rome, and although by then the capital of the Western part of the Empire had moved to Ravenna, the shock of this news must have been traumatic in Constan-

tinople, the heir to Roman greatness and Roman traditions. In addition, and much nearer to home, tribes of Huns had already crossed the Danube and begun to settle in what was held to be Byzantine territory.

The new land walls were built about two kilometres further inland than Constantine's original defences, and this extra territory was sufficient for the city's development for the rest of its history. Constructed of cut limestone with courses of thin bricks, they stood some ten metres (thirty-five feet) high, and were strengthened by almost a hundred towers in their length of about seven kilometres (four miles). They were built with such thoroughness and expertise that they may with some justice be said to have constituted the most successful system of fortifications ever constructed. Certainly for over a thousand years — from about 413 (although the outer wall and ditch were not actually completed until 447) until 1453 — these walls withstood all attacks and assaults from every kind of enemy. It was only by using the largest cannon the world had yet seen that the Turks were finally able to batter down a small section of the wall, and so ensure the success of their final assault. Although now cracked in many places as the result of numerous earthquakes, and having a jagged, uneven outline caused by the damage and depredations of over fifteen centuries, these walls provide the most vivid and evocative commentary on the strength and greatness of the city at its height, and on its later crumbling decline and ultimate defeat.

If there is one name, after that of Constantine, which is woven inextricably into the historic fabric of Byzantium, it is that of Justinian. From his accession in 527 until his death in 565 his enormous drive, political vision and genuine artistic imagination left an indelible and brilliant imprint on the life, institutions and culture of his capital. Besides important external military conquests, he made a number of far-reaching internal reforms, of which the most significant was the famous law code known as the 'Institutions of Justinian'. But it was in the appearance of his capital and its buildings that the Emperor's achievements were given their most permanent and impressive form.

Justinian was a passionate builder. All over the Empire he had buildings erected, often of unusual and experimental design. Even today these can still be seen, from the Sinai desert to the exarchate (province) of Ravenna. In Constantinople itself his first building was probably begun the same year that he came to the throne, and can still be seen today much as he left it. Tucked away down below the old hippodrome, close to the Sea of Marmara, the modern visitor will find the small Church of St Sergius and St Bacchus, for long now used as a mosque. Its relatively small scale and rather irregular — almost casual — plan conceal the originality of its design. For it was the exploration of ways in which a dome could be supported over a rectangular space that seems to have so fascinated Justinian and his builders. Here the dome is carried on eight piers, its surprising size made possible by the use of light building materials. It seems almost to float over the large central space of the nave.

It originally adjoined some of the buildings of the Great Palace, and it is possible to envisage it as a joint experiment between Justinian and his architects. Its haphazard design — no two walls are at right angles, and the dome is almost a metre wider in one dimension than the other and is not sited symmetrically within the walls — suggests that its originators were developing their ideas and techniques as the building proceeded. One thing is certain: no Roman from the ancient world would ever have experienced the particular spatial qualities that the interior of this building provides. Light and airy, it must have represented a completely new outlook on the possibilities that were open to a builder with the necessary imagination and vision. In the detail of its decoration there is also a new range of concepts at work; the melon-shaped capitals open a new chapter in Byzantine sculpture. Carved with immense subtlety and brilliance, they were formed with extensive use of drilling and under-cutting, so that their abstract and natural patterns appear almost as separate shells standing free from the load-bearing core of the capitals. Contemporary writers who described Justinian's buildings always emphasized the quality of lightness, and speak of the 'floating', detached feeling that his domed structures convey. It is hard not to conclude that there was one mind controlling all aspects of the work, and so providing this unity of both major forms and of the decoration of smaller units, and that this mind was the Emperor's.

The Turks have, with hindsight, aptly called this building 'Kücük Aya Sofia' — 'Little Hagia Sophia'. For probably even before St Sergius and St Bacchus was completed (the date of the smaller church is under debate), Justinian had begun the construction of what is arguably the most extraordinary and original building in the world: Hagia Sophia, or, as it became known, 'the Great Church'.

It was begun in 532, after the fifth-century structure had been burnt down in the course of serious riots, and from the beginning it was clearly intended to surpass all buildings that the world had yet seen. The vast interior is dominated by the dome, and the modern visitor as he stands beneath it can only concur with the Emperor Justinian, who, when the building was dedicated on December 26th, 537, is said to have exclaimed: 'Solomon, I have surpassed thee!'

How was this overpowering effect achieved? It must have been the result of a fascinating piece of teamwork. While the form of the dome, which is the pre-eminent feature of Hagia Sophia, had been known to the Roman world, it was here handled with an infinitely greater freedom and daring than had ever been attempted before. The very much smaller dome of St Sergius and St Bacchus must have been the testing ground which provided

Left: The construction of Hagia Sophia must have seemed to Justinian to be the crowning achievement of all his many architectural enterprises. The swelling forms of the apse, the eastern semi-dome and then the main dome, as they rise here one upon the other, must have provided an experience that no-one in the world had ever seen before. In its essentials, this view has not changed in over fourteen centuries.

Left: Now bare of all its furnishings, the huge central area of 'the Great Church' would have held richly decorated screens and hangings from the day of its dedication in 537. In this view of the nave, taken from the gallery reserved for the Empress as she attended the services with her entourage, if the later Turkish additions such as the mihrab and discs with texts from the Koran are ignored, the impression is perhaps more of how the interior would have looked as it neared completion, and just before it was in use.

Right: The extraordinary synthesis of rhythmically curving architectural forms, and the complex spaces which they enclose, are caught in this view of one of the exedras of the gallery. The fully developed intricacies of Justinianic sculpture and inlaid marble decoration, which reached their height in Hagia Sophia, are also very apparent.

the inspiration, and to some extent the model, for this huge enterprise. But while it now appears as something inevitable and pre-ordained, to Justinian and his builders the overwhelming scale of the dome of Hagia Sophia must always have had the character of a prodigious experiment. It may have been for this reason that Justinian's chief advisers on this project were not masons or master builders as the later Middle Ages knew the term. Rather, it looks as if he had conceived a vision of something so extraordinary and so outside the limits of known building construction that professional builders would have refused to believe that it could be achieved.

For by great good fortune some information is available concerning the two experts that Justinian employed for this, the major enterprise of his life. The contemporary writer Procopius gives their names as Anthemius of Tralles and Isodorus of Miletus, and — significantly — he refers to them as *mechanike* and *mechanopoios* respectively. The best translation for these terms is probably 'engineer', and it must have been mainly to the problem of engineering that they addressed themselves. They had the technical expertise to give substance to the over-lifesize vision of Justinian. Between them they provided the skills and understanding of mathematician, scholar, inventor, geometrician, physicist and engineer, and all these gifts were put to the service of the Emperor-builder.

Try to visualize the experience of a sixth-century Byzantine as he approached the Great Church — the name which so well expresses the people's pride in it. Coming from the direction of the Mese, he would have seen the western semidome swelling up to meet the forms of the main dome. This was probably lower and somewhat flatter in profile in its original form than it is now; part of the original dome collapsed in 558 (further indicating the experimental nature of the project), and the low drum, pierced by windows, and the more curved dome that it supports today, were only finished in 563. The visitor would not have seen very much of the massive substructure of the church before he entered a large atrium, or open courtyard, enclosed by porticos. This would have been the most 'classical' part of the whole building.

Crossing this he would have been very much aware of the huge bulk of the building 'soaring up to a height to match the sky', as Procopius expressed it. He would then have entered the narrow exonarthex (a long porch running across the full width of the church), and would have begun to glimpse the interior only after he had crossed this and was standing in the inner narthex which was much wider. From this, several more doors opened on to the vast nave. This first glimpse of the interior would have been breathtaking. Many writers have tried to express what this experience conveys, but no description touches the reality. The sixth-century Byzantine observer would have been aware of an even greater sense of mystery and semi-concealment than is the visitor today. Aside from the half-seen spaces beyond the main area of the nave, there would have been hangings between the columns of the galleries, and the altar would have been largely hidden by screening. Mosaics with much gold in them would have caught the flickering, reflected light of many lamps and tapers. The walls were clad with brilliantly patterned sheets of marble.

At no point in this building does an observer feel that he is seeing all of it at once. Always there are some parts that are hidden as others come into view. It is a mystifyingly complex arrangement of forms which, for Justinian's age, would have precisely mirrored the unseen mysteries and the allegorical and

Below and right: Interior views of Hagia Sophia. 'Who could speak of the beauty of the columns and stones with which the church is adorned? One might almost have found oneself in a meadow full of marvellous flowers, for one would exclaim equally at the purple of some of them, at the green of others, and at the glowing crimson of others, while yet others are gleaming white . . .' So wrote Justinian's biographer Procopius, and his poetic description of Hagia Sophia is still appropriate today. He continues: 'When anyone enters this church to pray, he is immediately aware that it is not by any human strength or skill that this work was made, but by the influence of God.'

This sixth-century column from Acre now in the Piazza San Marco, Venice conveys something of the immense richness and variety that could be found in buildings all over the Byzantine Empire at this time. While untold losses have reduced what can still be seen in Constantinople to a handful of examples, this trophy from a victory in 1285 by the Venetians has preserved by chance something of the brilliance of this great period.

poetic allusions of the liturgy and other services, as they were celebrated every day in the ceaseless, rhythmical cycle of the Orthodox Church's year.

It was by a superbly judged sequence of almost theatrical effects that Justinian was able to achieve the succession of impressions that the visitor to his church would have experienced. Technical descriptions of either the whole or any part of this incomparable building will fail to do it justice if this aspect of it is disregarded. Just as the relationship of one part to another changes as the visitor moves, so all the decoration was calculated to hover and shift with him. The marble patterning on the walls and piers, the silk curtains, the lace-like encrustation of the carved capitals, the glinting mosaics, all conspired to sustain the sense of endless and infinite variety within the whole. It must be significant that in Justinian's day none of the decoration of Hagia Sophia was figural — not even the mosaics; perhaps because it is natural for the eye to identify and be 'held' by images of the human figure, he apparently felt that abstract and floral ornament was more appropriate to the particular effect that he wished to create.

But even more important is it to visualize the interior of the building as it would have appeared when in use, with the great central area of the nave acting as a stage for the patriarch and his clergy during the enactment of the liturgy. The crowds of the faithful attending the services would have gathered in the aisles and galleries, and would have participated at a distance in the half-seen mysteries of the liturgy and other services. They would have glimpsed parts of the processions and movements of the clergy, they would have heard the clinking chains of the censers and chanting of the singers, smelt the incense as it rose to the mosaic-encrusted dome, and sometimes they might have glimpsed the Emperor and Empress taking their part in the grand, complex and restrained ritual of the Great Church.

Huge numbers of the people of the city attended major services, for very close to the Great Church was another building, second in size only to Hagia Sophia. This was the basilica dedicated by Constantine to St Irene, or 'Holy Peace', which was also burnt down in the riots of 532. This too was rebuilt by Justinian, though not to such an ambitious design as Hagia Sophia. It still stands today, and, although it was again remodelled after later damage, the visitor can still recapture something of the scale and grandeur of its appearance in Justinian's age.

The other great building that must have dominated the skyline of the city in the early centuries was the Apostoleion. It was built on higher ground than most of the rest of the city, and even today the 'Mosque of the Conqueror', constructed on the same site, stands out from the surrounding townscape. Contemporary records indicate that Constantine's building had become unsafe, so Justinian had had it pulled down. His rebuilding was on the same kind of 'Greek cross' plan, but with one of the arms of the cross slightly extended. The major difference between this building and its predecessor was that it was given no less than five domes — one over each of the arms and a larger one, raised on a drum over the crossing, in which there were windows. It was richly decorated with mosaic and sheets of different-coloured marble. There are several descriptions of this building which, as the mausoleum of the emperors, had a significance for the Byzantines second only to the Great Church. But the best indication of its appearance comes from quite a different source. On account of its fame it was copied a number of times during the Middle Ages, and the closest of the 'copies' is the Basilica of St Mark's, in Venice. To enter this church today, with its piers sheathed in marble, its vaults and five domes encrusted in a continuous glinting film of gold and coloured mosaic, and its floors formed from cut and inlaid marble, is certainly to undergo the same kind of architectural experience as would the sixth-century visitor to Justinian's Apostoleion.

Although it dates from the tenth century, this mosaic over the South Door of Hagia Sophia commemorates the two most important figures in the history of the early centuries of Constantinople. On the right Constantine is holding a model of the city in which great emphasis is given to the walls that he built, while on the left Justinian holds a model of Hagia Sophia itself; greatest importance is given to the dome, as this was the building's most famous and striking feature. Both the emperors hold these models as offerings to the Virgin, who was regarded as the protector of the city.

The Emperor's enormous energy and drive was also directed towards secular building. From his reign dates one of the great cisterns of the city, which can still be visited today — the 'Yerebatan Sarayi', or 'Underground Palace'. This structure must be almost exactly the same now as it was in the sixth century — an astonishing tribute to the planning and building skills of the age.

Also of fame throughout the known world was the imperial palace, much extended and embellished by Justinian; alas, only poetic descriptions of these works remain. Again, it is necessary to go to Italy to gain some idea of what, for example, the mosaics of Justinian and his Empress, Theodora were like. For in the Byzantine exarchate of Ravenna —'in effect a kind of colony of the Empire — time has been kinder to the mosaics of Justinian's age; it is ironic that what is today the most famous imagery of his whole reign was never seen by the Emperor, since he never set foot in Italy.

With the reign of Justinian the city of Constantinople truly came of age. Although the losses in art and buildings are enormous, enough is known or still survives for us to be able to picture the glories of the early centuries of this great and historic city.

THE EMPEROR
AND HIS COURT

As with so much of Byzantine culture, the concept of rule by an emperor can be traced back to ancient Rome. It was there that the Emperor Augustus (27 BC–AD 14) had established the principle, and although the Senate had originally retained considerable powers these had gradually dwindled; certainly by Constantine's age the Empire was an autocracy, with all the civil and military powers vested in one individual. It was this concept of the emperor as sole and absolute ruler that was to be sustained right through the eleven centuries of Byzantine civilization. The titles that successive emperors had adopted give us an idea of how they saw their position: *augustus* (and, for the empress, *augusta*) was used as a form of title throughout the Byzantine period. To this was later added the word *autocrator*, with its implication of absolute authority, and in the seventh century the Greek name for a king, *basileus* also began to be used. So when the full title of an emperor had to be given, as for instance in a prominent mosaic portrait in Hagia Sophia, an eleventh-century emperor, Constantine IX Monomachus, was called 'Constantine Monomachus, faithful Autocrator in Christ, King of the Romans'. This surely tells everything — an absolute monarch, trusting in God, ruling the *Romaioi* (as the Byzantines always persisted in calling themselves), and yet the whole title written in Greek!

But although the emperor in theory had absolute authority, the history of Byzantium, as indeed of all countries, has many examples of emperors who, for one reason or another, lost their grip on the throne. Illness, old age, incompetence or madness, as well as the political intrigues of rivals, could deprive the emperor of his power. In the case of the Byzantine emperor this was partly because an old concept still lingered on that, as in ancient Rome, the sovereignty was in some way in the possession of the people, and that they bestowed it on the emperor when he was crowned.

A grisly example of what could happen to an emperor who failed to maintain his authority is provided by the brief reign of Andronicus I Comnenus (1183–5). He came to power at a time when firm rule was needed to restore order after a period of chaos, during which a Western princess, Maria of Antioch, had been acting as regent for her son Alexius II. Andronicus was a man of violent and contrasting passions, who ruled with tyrannical disregard for the consequences of his actions. He genuinely wished to protect the exploited poorer classes, and to root out all corruption in the civil administration; he therefore ensured that all officials were properly paid, and punished all forms of extortion. To achieve this, however, involved losing the support of the powerful land owners in what was still a feudal system, and as a result Andronicus went in continual fear of

plots against his life. There were constant executions of powerful land-owning magnates who were suspected of planning to overthrow the Emperor in order to replace him with someone more sympathetic to their interests. Some of the best military leaders of the day were lost in this way, at a time when there were considerable external dangers. The accession of Andronicus had also been the occasion for a major massacre of Italian traders and merchants in Constantinople, with a withdrawal of all their trading concessions. The Normans, then occupying Sicily, immediately captured the island of Corfu, and then in 1185 captured and sacked Thessaloniki, which was the second city of the Byzantine Empire, and of great importance. When the people in Constantinople heard the news of this disaster, brought upon the Empire as a direct result of their Emperor's actions, they forgot the benefits he had brought them, and, remembering only his tyrannical behaviour and abuse of power, seized him and imprisoned him in chains in the Tower of Anemas, a prison in the city walls near to the Blachernae Palace. As he had lost the support of the army through his executions of military leaders, Andronicus was left to suffer what was perhaps the most gruesome fate of any of the Byzantine emperors. After spending several days in the stocks, where he had his teeth knocked out and was beaten constantly by all and sundry, one of his hands was cut off and he was tied to the back of a camel. He was paraded through the streets of the city in this way, one of his eyes was put out, and then he was brought to the Hippodrome and hung upside down between two columns. After further humiliation and torture he was pierced by the swords of three soldiers, while, according to the chronicler Nicetas, he constantly repeated the words 'Lord have mercy, why dost thou strike a broken reed?'

Thus, for all the God-given power with which the emperor was endowed, if by his actions he forfeited the basic goodwill and respect of the people, his fall could be more dramatic and complete than that of one of lesser rank. Indeed, of the eighty-eight Byzantine emperors, no fewer than twenty-nine died violent deaths.

In theory at least, the Byzantine emperor was elected; his electors were the Senate, the Army and the Byzantine people, and before he could be crowned these three bodies all had to acclaim him as their new emperor. Although this was largely a formality, it was this concept that lay behind the 'palace revolutions' that played such a large part in Byzantine history. Of the three elective bodies, the Senate was the weakest. It consisted of a large number of men whose sole qualification for being senators was that they had at some time held positions of authority in the city or the Empire, or that they were descended from someone who had done so. It was in effect the Byzantine Establishment, and so represented the interests of the more well-to-do and privileged citizens.

Of far more importance was the Army. In the tenth century, as in the twentieth, any ruler had to be supported by the military before he could reign with confidence. More will be said later of how the army worked,

Right: Chronicle of John Scylitzes, Madrid, cod. gr. S-3 fol. 217. v. Miniature showing Bulgar leader Alausonius receiving Deleanos in his palace, and gouging out the eyes of his rival. Blinding was a common way of coping with a contender.

Opposite: There is some uncertainty as to the date of this enamel on the Pala d'Oro in St Mark's, Venice. While the inscription says it is 'Irene, the most pious Augusta', the plaque itself may have formed a part of the new Pala ordered in 1105 by the Venetian Doge or it may have been added later, so it may be of Alexius I Comnenus' wife or the wife of his successor.

28

Above: This gold solidus was minted in 945, and the design shows the Emperor Constantine VII holding an orb surmounted by a cross. As in imperial portraits in mosaic, all the essentials of the regalia are accurately shown.

Right: This full-page frontispiece of a psalter shows the war-like Emperor Basil II dominant over the leaders of conquered Bulgarian tribes. Christ lends divine support, lowering a crown which is placed on Basil's head by an angel, while another angel supports his sphere, and warrior saints also give protection.

but any emperor's position ultimately depended on getting and maintaining its allegiance.

The third body that had to be satisfied before an emperor's rule could begin was the people of Constantinople. Although a huge and amorphous body, the people did collectively hold very great power, and on many occasions an emperor had to trim his policies to keep their favour. It was, for instance, in a spontaneous and corporate revolt against the heavy burden of Justinian's taxation that the people of the city rampaged over a large area around the palace in the famous Nika Riots of 532, and burnt down many buildings, including the fifth-century structure of Hagia Sophia.

So although he had such absolute power, with all financial and legal control in his hands, the Byzantine emperor had to be skilful at satisfying the various elements of the city and the Empire. One strategem that many emperors used in order both to maintain their own rule and to ensure a smooth transition of power, was that of co-opting other emperors, who would later succeed them. Most of the emperors were thus acclaimed and crowned in the lifetime of their predecessors, and it was this practice that formed the dynasties of Byzantine imperial families. Eventually, the dynastic idea came to appeal strongly to the Byzantines and a son could not succeed his father without this procedure being carried out. This policy gave the figure of the empress a power that the consorts of the Roman Caesars never possessed. She often had to act as regent until a child, already crowned, was old enough to rule, and at times even ruled the Empire as sole empress. Byzantine art shows many instances of an emperor and empress being crowned simultaneously by a figure of Christ, indicating divine approval of their joint rule.

As these procedures and rituals were so important to the Byzantines, it is interesting to see something of a Byzantine emperor's coronation. By great good fortune a first-hand account survives; an emperor of the tenth century, Constantine VII, wrote a long treatise called the *Book of Ceremonies* in which all the many rituals, services and processions of the court are described in great detail. Following is a summary of his account of the coronation ceremony.

All the Senate, the court dignitaries, leaders of the Army and Navy and a mass of the common people assembled in their most special parade

clothes. The emperor eventually emerged from the palace complex, accompanied by his personal staff, to receive the first greetings from the spokesman of those of patrician rank. After making his way through various official buildings surrounding the palace, the emperor went to an area known as the Hebdomon, where the most public part of his coronation took place. This consisted of his stepping on to a large circular shield, which was then raised up to at least shoulder height by a group of soldiers, so that all the surrounding crowds could see him. This ceremony had a direct link with the practice of the soldiers of ancient Rome, who acclaimed their new Caesar in just this way. The emperor then had further special robes put on, and entered Hagia Sophia. After lighting candles in two parts of the church and praying, he climbed into a pulpit, so that all could see the act of coronation. The patriarch, representing at this point the emperor's electors, then said prayers over the crown, and, ascending the pulpit steps, placed it on the emperor's head. Immediately all the congregation of the Great Church shouted three times: 'Holy, Holy, Holy, Glory to God in the highest and peace on earth. Many years to thee, O great king and autocrator!' The newly crowned emperor then sat upon a throne, and all the most important state dignitaries made obeisance to him. The *Book of Ceremonies* enumerates all twelve ranks of these officials. The emperor then returned to the pulpit to have more of the imperial regalia bestowed on him, and the singers in the choir of the Great Church started a long sequence of acclamations in which they alternated with the congregation:

> Choir: 'Glory to God who has made thee emperor.'
> People: 'Glory to God who has made thee emperor.'
> Choir: 'To the glory and exaltation of the Romans.'
> People: 'To the glory and exaltation of the Romans.'
> Choir: 'Many, many, many.'
> People: 'Many years on many years.'
> Choir: 'Many years to thee, the servant of God.'
> People: 'Many years to thee.'

After several hours, the service ended and the emperor emerged to be greeted by those who had not been able to enter the Great Church. Through-

This fourteenth-century mosaic of Theodore Metochites and Christ in the Church of St Saviour in Chora, or Kariye Djami, shows how orientalized the Byzantine court became under the Palaeologue dynasty. Theodore Metochites' main garment is made from stiff brocade, and his head supports a huge form of turban. Although he rose to the top of the Byzantine civil service, and became wealthy in the process, he represents a typical aspect of Byzantine piety; he is presenting to Christ a model of the church which he had restored and decorated, and in which he was to end his days, as a monk.

out the ceremony, every action and movement was carried out with a sombre dignity that conveyed the timeless grandeur of the event. No other institution in European history produced such a completely accepted fusion of the temporal and sacred powers in one individual as did the Byzantine state. His coronation gave to the emperor the position of a demi-god, holding not only the absolute authority of temporal office, but also that of the Viceroy of Christ. The Emperor Leo III (717–40) wrote to the Pope, 'I am both emperor and priest,' signifying his supremacy in spiritual as well as state matters.

While the ceremonies of the Byzantine court were susceptible to slow change and modification, the whole tenor of court life was essentially conservative. For instance, it was not until the Palaeologue dynasty that the practice of unction was introduced into the coronation ceremony. (This feature, absorbed into the ritual that was then almost a thousand years old, was in fact of Western origin, and still survives in the coronation of the British monarch.)

While the coronation ceremony was an exceptional one, there were others which involved the emperor almost every day; they must have taken up a considerable proportion of his life. These included rituals confined to certain parts of the palace, as well as processions the whole population could watch. The hippodrome was the focus of many of the more public appearances of the emperor, and the *Book of Ceremonies* devotes five chapters to describing them.

In addition to these duties the emperor would have been constantly involved in state business, the reception of foreign diplomats, negotiations with other powers receiving reports from leaders of the Army and Navy, dealing with ecclesiastical matters both of the city and throughout the Empire, and taking action on issues that concerned the finance of the state, and questions of law. Even with all these constant obligations, most emperors led their armies in battle. The support of the Army was always critical for the strength of an emperor's rule, and this was a way both of showing his leadership and of being sure of maintaining his control of the Army. The Byzantines would very rarely have seen their emperor leaving the city except at the head of his troops, and several emperors, such as Heraclius and Basil II, were highly successful military commanders.

But while the emperor's powers were absolute, he had to rely to an enormous extent on the administrative machinery of his court. If there was one single factor which could account for the survival of the Byzantine civilization for more than a millenium, it was surely its civil service. The Byzantine mentality seems to have been very effective at devising bureaucratic machinery that could deal with the major affairs of state, and adapt itself continuously to changing conditions. It was an immensely complex system, and one that was constantly developing; it involved questions of precedence at court functions, as well as titles and offices of state. These could be separate, or in some cases could be combined in one person.

From the highest and oldest of the court titles, such the *patrician* and the *magister*, which dated right back to the fourth century, the scale descended through later creations like the *kritai* and the *sekretikoi* to various *logothetes* and other officials. They all had different spheres of influence and responsibility, which from time to time fell into disuse, or were revised. As in court life at any period, titles were jealously guarded, and intrigues to climb the ladder of seniority were continuous.

A characteristic feature of the Byzantine court was the favoured position of eunuchs. They had existed as part of the emperor's entourage since the fourth century, and by the tenth they had become an important part of the system, having no less than eight distinct titles reserved for them. Their importance was due largely to the fact that by their nature they could not

On this gold scyphate (cup-shaped coin) from the reign of Romanus IV, the future Emperor Michael VII is shown standing between his two younger brothers, Andronicus and Constantine, who are holding orbs. The coin was issued between 1067 and 1071, and is a clear expression of dynastic strength.

be made emperors or found dynasties. Indeed, the son of a noble family might undergo castration in order to increase his chances of promotion, and to safeguard his future career at court; the emperor could be certain that he could entrust the most important and confidential duties to a eunuch, as the eunuch could never constitute an eventual threat in the form of a usurper. Not only the personal servants of the emperor and empress, but the main palace officials as well, tended to be eunuchs, and where there were two holders of the same rank, if one was a eunuch, it was he who took precedence. In the ninth and tenth centuries the most important of the eunuchs was the high chamberlain (or *parakoemomenos*) who was the senior minister of the whole Empire.

These officials could become very rich, and it is no doubt partly on this account that the portraits of a number of them have survived in works of art that they commissioned. As the Byzantine court became more orientalized, the robes of its officials changed from the classical toga of late antiquity to the stiff, patterned silk brocades that are seen clothing the members of the imperial family and their courtiers in later paintings and mosaics.

Looking at official portraiture of this kind, one becomes aware of the important part played by colour in the day-to-day life of the court. Just as writers delighted in describing the colours that they found in the various kinds of marble used in the building of Hagia Sophia or the Apostoleion, so the onlookers must have taken aesthetic pleasure in the brilliant spectacle of the robes of the emperor and his officials as they moved about the palace buildings in their innumerable processions.

But colour also had a symbolic function. In this respect, purple took absolute precedence, being reserved solely for imperial use. Not only was it used for the emperor's shoes, and other parts of his clothing, but even for the ink with which he signed state documents — the official called a *sebastokrator*, for example, had to sign his name in blue ink. As mentioned earlier, porphyry was the purplish marble that only emperors and their family could use. The term 'porphyrogenitus', meaning 'born in the purple', was applied to all the children of the empress, whose confinement took place in a room of the Great Palace that was lined with porphyry. This title carried no specific office or authority, but its prestige was enormous.

All this brilliance and richness of materials and colour can now only be glimpsed through the chance survival of works of art, or rare and tantalizing descriptions of Byzantine court practice. The only description extant of the famous porphyry chamber in the Great Palace occurs in a long history of Alexius I's reign, written by his daughter, Princess Anna Commena in the twelfth century:

> This purple chamber is a building of the palace which is square in shape from the floor to the beginning of the roof; it then takes on the form of a pyramid. It looks out on to the sea and the harbour, where there are the oxen and lions made from stone. The floor and walls are covered in marble — not the common sort, nor even the kind that is costly but obtainable, but that which the earlier emperors had carried off from Rome. This marble is, roughly speaking, purple, but it has small dots like white sand sprinkled all over it. It is because of this marble, I think, that our ancestors called the chamber 'purple'.

But of the accounts of the ceremonial life of the palace, the one that paints the most vivid picture is that written by an Italian bishop, Liutprand of Cremona. He was in Constantinople in 949 on official business, and when he was finally ushered into the throne-room of the emperor, this was his experience:

> Before the emperor's throne stood a tree; it was made of bronze and gilded all over. There were birds of different kinds in its branches,

and they also were made of gilded bronze; each sang its own kind of song, and together they formed a chorus. The emperor's throne was made with such skill that at one time it was level with the ground, and at another it was raised high up. It was guarded by what seemed enormous lions; it was not possible to say if they were of bronze or wood, but they were gilded all over. These opened their mouths and roared, moving their tongues and beating the ground with their tails. Here I was brought into the emperor's presence, leaning on the shoulders of two eunuchs. The lions roared when I appeared, and the birds sang according to their kind . . . Three times I lay prone at full length on the ground in the act of homage, and then I raised my head. Behold, the emperor, whom I had just seen before seated at ground level, now appeared to me dressed in different robes and raised almost to the ceiling of the palace. How it was done I could not imagine . . .

This gives a fascinating glimpse into the diplomatic world of the Middle Ages. We can surmise now that the throne on which the emperor was raised up to the ceiling was operated by hydraulic pressure, as probably were the birds who 'sang according to their kind'. The eunuchs by whom the foreign bishop was supported were no doubt trained to ensure that he did not raise his head until the process of elevating the throne was complete; in this way the maximum effect could be achieved. If a bishop from a relatively civilized country such as Italy was inclined to be overawed by this display, it is not hard to imagine the overwhelming impression that it would make on the chief of a semi-nomadic tribe, come to parley at the Byzantine court. This description also demonstrates the extent to which Byzantium had by the tenth century become Orientalized. Although its inhabitants still clung to the idea of being 'Romans', they had by now lived for three centuries as neighbours of Islam, and one can detect something of the Arab genius for mechanical invention in the engineering that contrived to make the gilded birds to sing, and the lions to roar and beat the ground with their tails.

CHURCH AND STATE
IN BYZANTIUM

One of the hardest transitions for a modern mind to make is in taking the imaginary view-point of a medieval man or woman. To empty one's mind of all the rational and scientific knowledge and attitudes which modern man is heir to is virtually impossible. And yet, if the outlook and behaviour of the Byzantines is to be at all understood, some such effort has to be made.

Most difficult for people today to understand, perhaps, is the preoccupation of the Byzantine people with questions of religion and religious controversy. It is as though, because the Byzantines had no opportunity for speculation and discussion on the sort of subjects that fill a modern newspaper, such as political changes and social and economic questions, their zest for enquiry spilled over into the world of religion. Again and again, particularly during the early centuries of Byzantium, the Empire was racked by bitter and protracted disputes over matters of the most minute theological detail. For example, one of these all-consuming questions, which recurred at several times in Byzantine history, concerned the nature of Christ. One party held passionately to the idea that in Christ's person there was only one nature, and that it was divine; this view was in opposition to the Orthodox teaching, which was that after the Incarnation, there were two natures, one divine and one human, in Christ's person. This subject was not only disputed by members of the Church, intellectuals, and leisured classes, who, one might assume, had time for such abstractions. Every man on the street was involved. Contemporary accounts suggest that these debates were of passionate concern to people. A man could even become involved in an argument about the precise relationship of Christ to God the Father while buying a loaf of bread! The strength of feeling that this controversy engendered had serious political consequences, threatening at one stage to divide the Empire. In order to prevent a damaging weakening of the Byzantine Empire in the face of the expansion by the Arabs in the seventh century a compromise formula was devised, whereby there were held to be two *natures* in Christ, but only one *will*. This largely political solution was imposed by the Emperor Heraclius (610—41), and held good for some ten years before itself being rejected as heretical (though this particular heresy, which became known as Monothelitism, was only officially and finally subdued at the Sixth Ecumenical Council held in Constantinople in 680).

One result of this widespread interest in theological speculation was the

This marble relief, now in St Mark's, Venice, depicts a particularly venerated icon that was kept in Constantinople. It is known as the Hodegetria, as the Virgin is pointing to the Christ child as if 'showing the way'.

Above: Initial O from an eleventh or twelfth-century illuminated manuscript, Athens, codex 2363, folio 2.v.

Opposite: Steatite is a soft stone, rather like soapstone, and it was used extensively by the Byzantines for small-scale relief sculpture, probably when ivory was scarce or unobtainable. Because of its fragility, much of the carving in steatite that has survived is in broken condition, although some fragments are of such fine quality that artists of the highest calibre must have worked in this medium. These two fragments are from reliefs which must originally have been of full-length figures of the Virgin and St Paul, and both probably date from the twelfth century. Their small scale indicates that they were intended only for private and personal use.

importance given in the Greek Church to the idea of Church councils. To a much greater extent than in the Western Church, these were regarded as the source of all theological truth. When a possibly heretical new attitude was being widely preached, the way to decide the matter was normally to hold a Church council. Constantine himself had initiated this idea with the first Church council of all, held at Nicaea (the modern Iznik) in 325, and this council had produced the Nicene Creed. This creed expressed all the beliefs and aspirations of the Church as it existed then, and Constantine hoped that it would provide the foundations for a reunited empire. It was both a summary of the main truths of the Gospel narratives, and a statement of the principal dogmas of the Church. There were seven major Church councils held between 325 and 787; these are the only ones which are held by both Eastern and Western Churches to have been genuinely 'ecumenical', in the sense that all parties had an equal voice in the proceedings. In many Greek churches today there are paintings of these councils in session, the implication being that the Orthodox doctrine which they established should always prevail in places of worship. In the Church of St Irene in Constantinople the tiers of semicircular seats, where bishops would sit in council, can still be seen.

It is easy to forget that when the Nicene Creed stated 'We believe . . . in one Holy Catholic and Apostolic Church', there was indeed only one Church. In the early fourth century the three senior Mediterranean bishoprics were Rome, Alexandria and Antioch. The Bishop of Byzantium was raised to being the Patriarch of Constantinople, but even then he was of a newer foundation than the bishoprics of Jerusalem and Athens. They all nevertheless adopted the Nicene Creed, and there was no question at this date of there being anything but 'one Catholic Church' — 'catholic' meaning 'universal'.

It was only later, as the centuries passed, that the polarization between 'Eastern' and 'Western' forms of Christianity began to occur. It was inevitable that the Italians and Greeks, being temperamentally so different, should wish in time to emphasize different aspects of the same basic faith; indeed, it is surprising that the differences which did develop were not greater, since the Roman genius for organization and government was in such striking contrast with the more philosophical and mystical attitude of the Greek mind. In fact, the differences were confined mostly to very small points, with only two major areas of persistent conflict.

One of these, predictably, was the question of the primacy of the pope. As the Western parts of the Empire were lost to Byzantium he, as the Bishop of Rome, became responsible for the control of Western Christendom, and in the early centuries he was appealed to by Constantinople and Alexandria when they disputed priority in ecclesiastical matters. The claim of the papacy to be in direct succession to St Peter could not be matched by Byzantium, and there were occasions when the pope even claimed to have authority over Church councils. It could be said that this one dispute over the position of the papacy lay at the root of all the conflicts which eventually divided the Eastern and Western Churches.

The second important dispute illustrates well the ability of minor points of theology to cause major political storms. It concerned the single Latin word '*filioque*', meaning 'and the son'. This word, which did not appear in the Nicene Creed, was inserted into the Creed by the Western Church, altering the meaning considerably. The relevant sentence as used in the Western liturgy, became: 'We believe . . . in the Holy Spirit . . . which proceeds from the Father *and the Son.*' This doctrine of the so-called 'dual progression' of the Spirit was confirmed in the West by the sixth century, and remained one of the most serious points of difference between Rome and the Orthodox Church. It was still a major cause of dissension at the

Council of Florence in 1439, when union between Rome and Constantinople was a vital political issue in the face of the approaching Turkish menace; the best theologians in the world debated the question then for several months.

The other differences between the Greek and Roman Churches were less important. One concerned the celibacy of the clergy, celibacy having been the normal practice in the West from the earliest centuries. In the Greek Church priests and deacons have always been expected to be married before ordination, although they could not marry after. Another point of difference was the kind of bread used at the Eucharist; the Greek Church used leavened bread, while the Roman Church used unleavened. While these differences initially developed without anyone's having a full realization of the problems that they would cause, they eventually became insuperable barriers to genuine unity. The final breach, or Schism, between the Eastern and Western Churches only took place officially in 1054, when a particularly powerful Greek Patriarch, Michael Cerularius, brought it about largely for reasons of personal aggrandizement. But the two sides had by that time become so entrenched in their differing practices that the Schism was hardly more than an acknowledgement of a state that already existed. While there were many subsequent attempts to bring about a reunion, none of them succeeded in bridging the gap between the traditional views that had built up over the centuries.

Once questions of theology had been decided in Byzantium, however, they had to be seen to be imposed, and for this the Byzantine Church was very well organized. The Church in Constantinople remained to the last closely modelled on the organization of the secular Empire. Just as this was heir to the Roman genius for clear-cut administrative practice, so the Church too built its structures on the same lines. At the summit of the pyramid was the patriarch in Constantinople; under him came the metropolitans and archbishops of the large cities and major provinces; answerable to them were the many bishops, who in turn controlled the local village priests. Unlike the Western Church, however, the Byzantine Church made an important distinction between the humble priests (or 'popes') and the higher clergy. The priests were supposed to be married, in order to obviate temptation and scandal, whereas the higher clergy — bishops and above — were all recruited from the monasteries, and so were celibate. The clever son of an ambitious family might well become a monk, therefore, in order to be available for eventual high office. Advancement within the Church was one of the ways open to citizens of any social standing, and was thus genuinely democratic. There were large numbers of monasteries in Constantinople, and citizens would have been familiar with the sight of monks in the streets and forums of the city. For most of the life of Byzantium there would have been many thousands of monks living in the city at any one time.

With such great significance being attached to questions of belief, it was obviously important that the emperor's personal outlook be above suspicion: he, of all people in the state, had to be strictly orthodox. This religious aspect even entered into the titles of some emperors. Thus, for example, in the mosaic of the tenth-century Emperor Alexander in Hagia Sophia, the inscription reads: 'Lord, help thy servant, the orthodox, faithful Emperor.'

The importance of church affairs was also apparent in the tensions inherent in the relationship between Church and state. While it was true that the emperor had absolute ultimate authority in all matters, it was possible for an ecclesiastical leader to gather so much personal support and even adoration from the populace that even an emperor would have to weigh up the position very carefully before opposing him. Because of this an emperor would be very careful in selecting a patriarch. In theory, the patriarch was elected by the bishops, in fact he was the emperor's choice.

The Epitaphios of Thessaloniki, shown here and on the following pages, is one of the greatest works of Byzantine textile art. Discovered in a church in Thessaloniki in 1900, it provides a touchstone for the handling of gold and silver thread with silk thread of other colours, by which all other Byzantine embroidery can be judged.
The use of the liturgical epitaphios was developed in the fourteenth century, when officiating priests used it in the 'Great Entry'. Contemporary frescoes show that the epitaphios was laid on the heads and shoulders of two or three priests, who then walked with it in that position, carrying the eucharistic bread and wine towards the altar.

Opposite: Most epitaphia have only representations of the body of the dead Christ lamented by angels, and sometimes by other figures such as the Virgin and some of the apostles and evangelists. This epitaphios is unique in that it also contains depictions of the communion of the apostles, with Christ administering the wine in the left-hand section, and the bread in the right. This emphasizes the liturgical use of the epitaphios in the service of the eucharist. The extended sequence of subjects makes the Thessaloniki epitaphios unusually long for its width (2.00 metres long by 0.70 metres wide), most being squarer in format.

This partnership could be a difficult one. While the emperor needed the patriarch's acquiescence in many church matters — it was after all the patriarch who placed the crown on the emperor's head at his coronation — the patriarch was even more dependent on the ultimate protection that the emperor could provide. In the last resort, the emperor could depose a patriarch who opposed his policies simply by stacking a Church synod with bishops of whose support he was sure. Indeed, it was thanks to effective, if rather unedifying, practices such as this that the Byzantine state was able to survive for so many centuries. The ultimate sanction that a patriarch could hold over an emperor was excommunication. Sometimes the threat of this alone was sufficient to bring about a change of heart in the emperor, as when the Patriarch Polyeuctus refused to crown the murderer John Tzimisces. Unless he fulfilled particular conditions he would be excommunicated, and so become ineligible for coronation. Tzimisces did as he was told. At other times the threat was actually carried out, although this was usually followed by the deposition and exile of the patriarch. An occurrence of this kind took place in the tenth century during the struggle between the Patriarch Nicholas Mysticus and the Emperor Leo VI. The Emperor, already three times widowed, wished to contract a fourth marriage. In canon law, even three marriages were forbidden, and very strong pressures had to be brought to bear on the Patriarch to sanction the scandal of a fourth. Leo would probably not have persisted had not the beautiful Zoe Carbonopsina, his intended bride, presented him with a son and heir out of wedlock; the birth took place in 905. The Patriarch agreed to baptise the child, but refused to perform the parents' marriage rites unless they agreed to subsequently live apart. They would not agree to this, and got another priest to perform the marriage ceremony. The scandal of this action, for the people of Constantinople as well as the Patriarch, was such that Leo VI was excommunicated, and was actually prevented from entering Hagia Sophia to worship at the Christmas and Epiphany services in 906–7. Leo then decided to depose Nicholas Mysticus; he eventually achieved this, but not without asking for the help of the Pope in Rome, whose authority, along with the authority of the Eastern patriarchs of Alexandria and Antioch, was still at that date necessary for the deposition. The Emperor's fourth marriage was eventually legitimized, and his son made a true Porphyrogenitus. But even then the Patriarch had the last word; on Leo's death his brother Alexander became emperor, Zoe was banished to a convent, and Nicholas Mysticus was installed again as patriarch. For the most part, though, emperors did not intervene in church matters unless they had good reason to.

There would always have been a very clear external distinction for all

Church figures. Monks, nuns, priests, bishops, archbishops, metropolitans — they all had their particular forms of dress, and would never have appeared at any time clothed as laymen. In the streets of Constantinople they would have been readily identified by the black sobriety of their robes and head-gear. Although there were changes in ecclesiastical dress over the centuries, black was the normal colour of all outer garments, with variations in cut and form indicating the position and status of the wearer. But it was a very different matter when ecclesiastics put on their robes for worship. Just as their churches had relatively undecorated and severe exteriors, with colour and richness of decoration reserved for inside, so the monks and clergy were transformed when they put on their robes of office for ceremonies and services. A whole range of vestments and insignia were developed by the Byzantines, each with its own decorative qualities, function and symbolism. These were familiar and respected features of the church life of Constantinople and the rest of the Empire, and were viewed with pride and even

The emotional content of the whole epitaphios, with the angels grieving over Christ's body, is emphasized by the brilliantly controlled composition and supremely effective handling of the medium.

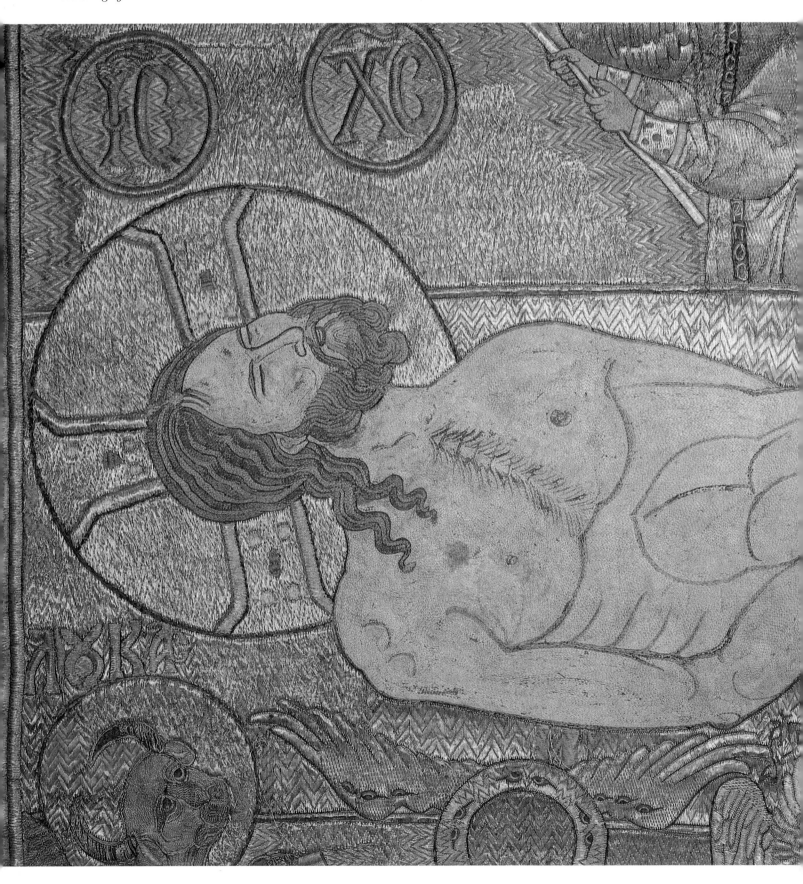

held in great reverence by all the population.

For bishops, the most prominent garment was the *phelonion*, which was the equivalent of the chasuble in the West; it covered the liturgical under-garment, the *sticharion*, and in the Middle Ages it was decorated all over with crosses. Because of this it was known as a *polystavrion*, and it is prominent in paintings of Church councils and other assemblies. Another item worn by a bishop was the *epigonation*, which was a stiffened square of richly embroidered material, hanging from the girdle. He also wore an *omophorion* as part of his insignia, which took the form of a long narrow strip of cloth decorated with crosses, and thrown loosely round his shoulders. He carried a staff as he walked.

The vestments of deacons and priests were less complex. Under his *phelo-nion* a priest wore an *epitrachilion* — a stole — which was placed round his neck after he had put on the *sticharion*. A deacon just wore an *orarion* over his left shoulder — a single strip of embroidered cloth, which became the *epitrachilion* when he was made a priest.

The impressive and colourful spectacle that these robes presented would have been further enhanced by other regalia used in the liturgy and other services. The cloth covering the altar, and the decorated veil spread over the vessels, with the richly coloured curtains of the screen before the altar and the other hangings beneath the icons and between columns of the church, all contributed to the atmosphere of subdued splendour that surrounded the celebration of the mysteries. The setting was completed by the lavish use of hanging lamps and wax tapers; like everything connected with the Byzantine Church, these had both a symbolic and a practical part to play in the ritual.

This only represents the visual side of Church ceremonial, however. Mingling with the smoke from the lamps would have been the aromatic clouds of incense sent up by the censers; the experience of this smell would have been confined to churches, so forming a strong association for the Byzantine worshipper. The rhythm of the censers' swinging was emphasized by the ringing of the small bells which were often attached to them, the sound combining with the clinking of their chains.

One of the great glories of the Byzantine age was its music. No description of the context of Byzantine Church ceremonial would be complete without reference to it. Music was extremely important to the Byzantines, and represented for them a link with their Greek origins. An eleventh-century author, Michael Psellus, writes of music as having a power which emanates out to everything; its effect is so strong, he says, that 'mastering rhythms and melodies can be directed to educating the character'. No instruments were ever allowed inside a Byzantine church, and to this day, all Church music is solely vocal, and quite unaccompanied. This is due to the strong traditional belief, going back to ancient Greece, that music was capable of exciting the passions of men and women to violent excesses. The Byzantines had quite a wide variety of instruments that were used for private and secular enjoyment, and for processions, but on arrival at a church door they were left outside.

Liturgical singing probably underwent more drastic change and development during the Byzantine age than other aspects of worship, but it was always given great importance. As the services developed into the forms in which we now know them, new chants and melodies were added to the traditional stock available to the singers. Some composers were given the highest honours, and some, like the most famous of all Byzantine hymnographers, Romanos, were even made saints.

So it is not hard to understand why the churches and church services were of such overwhelming importance for the Byzantines. The central act of the liturgy gathered together all the diverse strands of their complex origins, weaving them into a timeless and unending tapestry of spiritual and physical experience. In its complete and final form the liturgy conveyed, through an infinite sequence of visual and verbal imagery, poetic allegory and scriptural allusion, the Byzantine view of the Christian universe. For each day of the Church's year there was a prescribed order of service, in which individual saints would be commemorated or, as the year unfolded, the major feasts would be celebrated. Through this preordained and intensely emotive ceremony, and through the earthly mediation of the clergy, the patriarch and ultimately the emperor, the Byzantine worshipper would feel himself linked to the Godhead. It was in this way that the Byzantines saw their existence in this world as justified and fulfilled, whatever their stations in life might be.

Another feature of life in Constantinople that would have been of great interest and importance to the Byzantines was the part played by relics. From the early centuries it had been held that objects which had been associated with a saint, or indeed the material remains of a saint's body after his death, were worthy of special veneration. Relics were brought to the city from the time of its first foundation; whole churches were built to house them. They were enshrined in golden reliquaries encrusted with precious stones, and were frequently displayed both during services and in public processions through the streets of the city. To touch a relic, or even to glimpse it from a distance, was to absorb something of its virtue and protective powers.

Of the thousands of relics kept in Constantinople, pride of place went to a few supremely important ones. The city held the robe of the Virgin Mary, which was regarded as its safeguard and was paraded on the city's walls when they were under attack. Also there were Old Testament relics, some of which Constantine had enclosed in the base of his column when the city was founded; among these were the axe which Noah had used to build the ark, and the stone from which Moses had drawn water in the wilderness. But it was mainly the relics directly connected with New Testament narratives that were regarded as having the most extraordinary powers. Most important were the Virgin's robe, and some of her milk. Then there were the

Above: Bindings of great richness and brilliance were reserved for just a few liturgical books. This bookcover, probably of the ninth century, was almost certainly looted in the Fourth Crusade of 1204. The medallion in the bottom left-hand corner is clearly a replacement.

Opposite: The plan of the eleventh-century basilica of St Mark's, laid out in the form of a cross, with domes sited over each of the arms of the cross, and with a fifth larger one over the crossing, was copied from the Church of the Apostles in Constantinople, and provides superb evidence of the close ties the Venetians had with Constantinople. Containing much booty from the Fourth Crusade, St Mark's provides the nearest experience one can have of one of Byzantium's most famous churches.

crown of thorns worn by Christ on the cross, the nails, some of Christ's blood, the sponge and reed used at the crucifixion, and the stone slab on which Christ was laid in the tomb. These would have been the subject of extreme veneration by all Byzantines. Besides these major relics, there was a host of minor ones ranging from the body of St Andrew through the teeth of St Christopher and St John the Baptist, to the arms of St Clement and St Barnabas, the finger of St Nicholas, the knee of St Simeon and the foot of St Cosmas.

This great reverence for the physical remains of the Virgin, Christ, and the saints was shared by the whole medieval Christian world. The bodies of the saints had become, by the sanctity of their precious lives, temples of the Holy Spirit. The connection between the temple of the body, manifest in these remains, and the temple which was the church itself was strengthened by the ruling of the Second Council of Nicaea, held in 787, that no church should be consecrated which did not contain or possess some relics.

The presence of all these relics within the walls of Constantinople sheds further light on how the Byzantines saw their Church and city in relation to the rest of the world. Many of these objects — and all of the most important ones — had originated in the Holy Land. After the death of Mahomet and the subsequent rapid rise and expansion of Islam in the seventh century, Constantinople tended to see herself as the guardian of the whole Christian tradition in the East. It was natural that the city which Constantine had dedicated to the Virgin should hold the most precious of her relics. One relic exists even to this day, in the Treasury of the Topkapi Museum in Istanbul. It has survived the plunder of the Fourth Crusade in 1204, the sack of 1453, and over five centuries of Turkish rule. Encased in a silver arm, with a small window in the back of the hand, it bears a Greek inscription: 'With this hand was baptised Jesus, the Lamb of God.' It is the hand of John the Baptist.

The entire world as the Byzantines knew it was subject to the control of God. Through prayer to Him, to the Virgin and to the saints who had led lives of particular devotion, they believed it was possible to influence the course of history. In particular, they regarded the Virgin as taking particular care of Constantinople, guarding it against their enemies, and warding off where possible all natural disasters. Any calamity that befell the city — or indeed that befell any individual — had been permitted to occur by the Almighty; even prayer to the Virgin to intercede with Christ on behalf of the city had not been successful. The evil that had befallen the city must therefore be the result of some transgression. It was this sense of the predetermination of all events by some absolute and higher power that lay behind the Byzantines' lack of interest in scientific speculation or discovery. Even the Grand Logothete of the Treasury, Theodore Metochites, a renowned scholar who lived into the 1330s, when he wrote an introduction to the study of astronomy, accepted all the major precepts of Ptolemy. In 1200 years no major advance had been made in this field; the concept of scientific observation and analysis of the natural phenomena of the world was one that was foreign to the Byzantine mind.

It was possible to interpret the survival of Constantinople for so many centuries as a direct result of this protection by divine powers. The Arabs, as they expanded across North Africa and into Syria in the seventh century were a major threat, but they never succeeded in breaching the walls of the 'God-guarded city'. Surely this was a sign of divine approval; God was saving the stronghold of Christianity from the infidel. Why else should He have entrusted to the care of Constantinople so many of the relics from the land of the New Testament if He had not ordained that the city should be their custodian? For while politically Constantinople was always seen to be the New Rome, in the eyes of its Churchmen it was also the New Jeru-

Opposite: Although this relic of the hand of St John the Baptist appears to be of a form that is more commonly met with in Western Europe, the Greek inscriptions on it suggest that it is of Byzantine origin.

Right: This relic is of a large part of the skull of St John the Baptist, and its mounting and cover are of a richness reflecting the great veneration in which it was held. The inscription shows that the work is Bulgarian, so it may have been a gift to the Byzantine court.
These are among the few relics surviving of the many hundreds that were once kept in Constantinople's churches.

Below: This fresco painting of 'the Harrowing of Hell', Anastasis, is in the apse of the large side chapel of the Kariye Djami, which Theodore Metochites had built on to the church in the early fourteenth century.

salem. To possess the cross of Christ (found, after all, by Constantine's mother) and part of the Holy Sepulchre was, it would seem, tantamount to possessing Jerusalem itself. The Byzantines set little store by the worldly, physical reality that even then dominated so much of Western thought and action. Rather, they very readily and easily made the transition from the day to day matters of life in this world to abstract concern with life in the hereafter. Indeed, theology and religious dogma were expressions of the national consciousness. A people that could endow relics and images with such power, and be moved to great passions over the minutiae of theological debate, clearly attached great importance to things of the spirit. That is why, in Byzantium, the affairs of the Church were so tightly interwoven with those of the state.

LATER
DEVELOPMENT
OF
CONSTANTINOPLE

In many ways the Fethiye Djami, dedicated to St Mary Pammakaristos, is typical of many of the churches of Constantinople which have not survived. It was founded during the Comnene period, had additions and embellishments made to it during the thirteenth and fourteenth centuries, and survived the Turkish conquest, being turned into a mosque in 1587. It is exceptional chiefly for the fact that from 1455 until it was taken over by the Turks it was the seat of the Greek Patriarchate, and so for that period was one of the most politically important churches in the world. This view of the apse, now restored, shows well the highly decorative effects achieved by masons in the later Byzantine period.

Just as with the walls of Theodosius the city reached its natural limits as far as its immediate territory was concerned, so the buildings of Justinian established a set of architectural concepts that were to provide inspiration for Byzantine builders for centuries afterwards. There was no attempt made ever again to match the scale of Hagia Sophia, but later generations of builders continued to experiment with the building forms which he had initiated; the appearance of the city was certainly dominated by these ideas.

While the scale of achievement reached in Justinian's age was never to return, in other ways the culture of Byzantium reached new heights in the tenth and eleventh centuries, under the Macedonian and Comnene dynasties. But these achievements were only possible because of the protection given to the city by its defences which again and again proved too much for the attackers. In 626 Constantinople was besieged by Avars and Slavs, and over several years in the 670s the Arabs laid annual siege to the walls, as they did again in 717. In 813 the Bulgars under their leader Krum were repulsed, and again in 922 under Simeon. The Russians made the first of many attacks in 860, and later, in the eleventh century, tribes of Uzes and Patzinaks had to retire defeated.

Internally, there were also economic and political difficulties, and violent power struggles, with usurpers exploiting the weak condition of the state. Between 711 and 717 no less than three emperors came and went in quick succession before the throne was mounted by the powerful figure of Leo III; he initiated a new dynasty — the Isaurian — and restored some stability to the city.

While there must have been recurrent phases of building and reconstruction during these middle centuries of the Byzantine period, building which included secular housing, roads, harbours and minor palaces — as well as additions to the Great Palace — very little has survived the centuries of later Turkish rule. Virtually all that remains in the city from the later centuries of its greatness is a scattered group of church buildings; they have all been turned into mosques, and some have fallen into such a ruined condition that they have been unusable for any purpose for many years.

It might be thought that these churches were the only survivals of a broader group of buildings of all kinds, that they had not suffered the fate of all other Byzantine buildings because of their religious functions both before and after the Turkish conquest; had other kinds of building survived, they might also have exhibited the brilliantly inventive architectural qualities that the churches display.

This is probably not the case, however. Whenever the exploits of rich Byzantine patrons — and even the emperors and empresses — were recorded

*A great emphasis on the importance of
a variety of colours and richness of materials
is a characteristic of the decoration of
buildings in the Paleologue period, as can
be seen in this interior view of St Mary
Pammakaristos (Fethiye Djami).*

by contemporary chroniclers, it is clear that the available resources for building were mainly channelled into the construction and decoration of churches. To a very large degree Byzantine architecture — in the sense of the most advanced and experimental kinds of building — was church architecture. Just as the predominant expression of the genius of the Romans can be found in their road systems, fortifications and structural engineering, so the Byzantines found their chief outlet for architectural expression in innumerable church buildings, often quite small, but always individual, subtly playing on established principles while exploring new spatial ideas.

Here is how a biographer, writing about a generation later, described the most important activities of the Emperor Basil I, whose reign of ten years ended in 886:

> Between his war-like endeavours which he often, for the sake of his subjects, directed to a good end like a president of athletic contests, the Christ-loving Emperor Basil, by means of continuous care and the abundant supply of all necessary things, raised from ruin many holy churches that had been rent asunder by prior earthquakes or had entirely fallen down or were threatening immediate collapse . . . [Here follow accounts of a repair to the western arch of Hagia Sophia and of a repair and buttressing of the Church of the Apostles.] Also the Holy Church of the Mother of God at the Pege [a church built by Justinian at a spring of water where he had been cured of a kidney ailment] that had decayed and shed its pristine beauty he renewed and wrought more splendid than before. And similarly the other Church of the Mother of God called the Sigma that had suffered a grievous collapse he rebuilt from the foundations and made it more solid than the previous one. He furthermore rebuilt from the foundations the church of the first martyr Stephen at Aurelianae that had fallen to the ground . . . And furthermore he deemed worthy of his solicitude and raised from ruin the big church of the martyr Mocius, which had suffered many fractures and whose sanctuary part had fallen down and crushed the altar table. And the church of Andrew, the first-called among the apostles, which stands close to St Mocius in a westerly direction, and which had crumbled to pieces from neglect, he raised to its ancient beauty by means of proper measures. Furthermore the Church of St Romanus . . . and of St Anna in the Deuteron . . . and of the martyr Aemilianus . . . and the Holy Church of the martyr Nazarius . . .

[From: C. Mango: *The Art of the Byzantine Empire 312—1453*]

The biographer enumerates no less than fourteen churches which Basil I rebuilt or restored. Only then does he go on to describe the major new foundation of Basil's reign, the Nea Ekklesia, or 'New Church', which was an important source of architectural style and ideas for several generations of builders in Constantinople. This, with a smaller but equally famous church called St Mary of the Lighthouse, set the character of much of the more advanced building in the city during the tenth and eleventh centuries, and even later.

It is important to realize how great was the number of religious buildings in Constantinople, if any feeling for the atmosphere of the city in these centuries is to be achieved. There are documentary or historical references to no less than 345 monasteries and convents, and to over 500 churches in the city and its immediate neighbourhood. This figure must be conservative, however, as it is only derived from the chance survival of written sources. The precise figure can never now be known, but the Spanish traveller, Ruy de Clavijo, who was in Constantinople in 1403, and who gives a fairly sober and factual account of what he saw, ends his description of the city by saying: 'They say even now that it holds within its circuit 3000 churches, great and small.' While this in turn is probably an exaggeration, it shows what a strong impression churches and other religious buildings made on the visitor. Such a huge number of religious foundations would, of course, have given a very particular character to the city, and also provides ample evidence regarding the interests of the hundreds of individual founders of these buildings.

From accounts written by people who saw these churches when they were still in use, and from the reflections of them that can still be seen in such buildings as the Budrum Djami, Fenari Isa Djami or the Gül Djami, it is possible to get quite a clear idea of the general character of the hundreds of churches which furnished the city over these centuries.

The typical 'middle Byzantine' church in Constantinople tended to be quite high in relation to its ground area, and its whole appearance was dominated, both inside and outside, by one or more domes. This feature had become an essential part of Byzantine church building, and could be found in other prestige architecture, such as palaces, as well. Most of these churches were quite small, and to modern eyes would seem rather dark inside. It is clear that great ingenuity was used to achieve variety in wall surfaces, and where possible niches and recesses were introduced to break up any large flat areas of wall. This tendency to undulating and fragmented architectural surfaces, with swelling, curving forms rising up to a broad cupola, was very evident on the exterior, but it was probably developed to

A brilliant development of monumental art during the Palaeologue period was that of the fluted dome, clad with gold mosaics. This south dome of the inner narthex of Kariye Djami appears almost to hover over the spectator, as some mosaic facets are always reflecting light while others are in shadow. An image of Christ Pantocrator is at the apex of the dome, while forty-six ancestors of Christ are shown in two zones below. Theodore Metochites wrote that in the decoration of his church he wanted 'to relate in mosaics and paintings how the Lord Himself . . . became a mortal man on our behalf'.

Ivory carving was one of the widely practised luxury trades in Byzantium, and triptychs such as this were highly valued. Their size indicates that they were intended only for private devotional use. The form of that shown here, which dates from the tenth century, is very typical, with a larger central panel showing a major scene (frequently, as here, the Crucifixion) flanked by the two folding panels depicting saints of particular significance to the owner. There was also frequently a liturgical basis for the sequences of saints that appear in this kind of context.

complement the treatment of the interior. This was always heavily decorated. While poorer churches had more modest treatment, with lesser quantities of rich marble, their upper areas being covered with painted decoration, more expensive foundations made lavish use of large amounts of marble, and of mosaics and other decorative surfaces. The reflecting qualities of the mosaics, when applied to the curving and faceted walls and cupolas, tended to make the decoration take on a life of its own. The Byzantine writers who describe these interiors often talk of the 'floating' character of the figures in the mosaics, as they appeared to hover apart from their gold background, and even describe in this way the qualities of a whole mosaic-encrusted cupola. Even to a modern, scientifically informed eye, mosaic interiors where they have survived can create sensations of a secondary diffused reality; how much more to the medieval Byzantine worshipper, seeing these shapes through the flickering smokey light of a dimly lit and crowded atmosphere, would the effect have been that of a different realm of reality from the one he had left behind when he came in from the street.

So as the centuries passed the character of the various districts of the city developed, with the domes of these many smaller churches showing prominently above the huddled collections of poorer shops and houses. The Byzantines were always prepared to add to or reinstate existing buildings, and modern excavations have shown that reconstruction was widespread. Throughout its history the city kept the basic form on which it had been founded, with the Mese always remaining the chief thoroughfare. This was not in fact very wide — probably about five metres (some fifteen feet) — and was lined on either side by covered colonnades. It was here that the main shops and booths of the traders could be found, although as different areas were built up they no doubt developed their own commercial life. If the principal street was only five metres across, the alleys running through the areas of poorer housing must often have been so narrow that even the passage of a horse and cart would have been difficult.

*Above: Eleventh or twelfth-century pottery
bowl, with ship in incised underglaze.
Considering the quantity of pottery that must
have been in use in Constantinople,
tantalizingly little has survived, and much
that has is in fragmentary condition.
Virtually none has been found that gives
a clue to the kind of pottery that must have
been in use before the ninth century.*

*Right: Although so little has survived of
the secular art of Byzantium, it should not be
ignored in any reconstruction of the
appearance of the city. This relief carving of
a lion devouring a gazelle, which would
have adorned a rich man's palace, probably
dates from the ninth or tenth century.
The formalized treatment of the animals
may owe something to a knowledge of
Islamic art.*

The modern visitor to the city is often surprised at its sheer size, and during all periods there were open areas where vegetables and other crops could be grown dividing the districts where houses had been built. In the last centuries of its life, Constantinople must have seemed more like a collection of ruined villages than a major city.

As the city expanded, various of the emperors built new palaces in different parts of the city. Beside the large new palace called the Manganae constructed, with much rich decoration, by Basil I between Hagia Sophia and the Sea of Marmara, there was a palace built by the Emperor Theophilus (829—42) on the Asiatic side of the Bosporus. This was apparently very extensive, and owed much in its design and decoration to the arts of Islam; although only some substructures now remain, it probably marked a high point in the influence of Arabic taste on the Byzantine court. In all likelihood it was also under Theophilus that a game very like polo was imported from Persia; this still being played in the vicinity of the Great Palace during the reign of Basil I.

But it was the palace at Blachernae, right against the land walls, where they run down to the Golden Horn, that was to become the favourite residence of the emperors. It already existed in Theophilus' day, as he is known to have added to it, and Alexius I Comnenus made further improvements; his grandson, Manuel II, completely rebuilt it in the twelfth century. Probably by this time, or not long afterwards, the huge, rambling complex of buildings that made up the Great Palace was falling into such disrepair that it was gradually abandoned by the emperor and his court. Today its site is marked only by the warren of small streets and ramshackle Turkish houses where the land falls away towards the Sea of Marmara.

The appearance of the city during these later centuries was also affected by natural hazards. Besides the danger from fires, which, as in any medieval city, were always occurring, the area has been continuously subject to earthquakes. Those of 542 and 554 had been sufficiently severe to damage the walls of Theodosius, and a further severe shock in 558 damaged Hagia Sophia and many of the city's other buildings. Hardly a century seems to have passed without this natural catastrophe striking the city, and sometimes quite frequently within a few decades there was considerable damage from this cause — three earthquakes occurred in less than sixty years in 975, 1032 and 1033. These disasters — unpredictable and terrifying in their effects — must in the end have induced a certain fatalism in the Byzantines, yet they still made good the damage the earthquakes caused to their defences, however low the finances of the empire might have been. A particularly severe tremor caused such havoc to the land walls in 1344 that their whole length needed repair.

Misfortune of a different kind was visited on the city in 1348, when, as throughout the rest of Europe, the Black Death decimated the population. The plague had originated in central Asia, and was carried through the Crimea to the Aegean, so that Constantinople was one of the first European cities to be struck by it. Indeed, it was probably the Genoese galleys that traded with the city that carried the plague into Western Europe. With all these possible disasters that might at any time strike their city, the Byzantines would also have had in mind the story of an even more unexpected hazard — icebergs. According to the historian Theophanes, the winter of the year 764 was so severe that the Black Sea froze up to a hundred miles from the shore; snow built up on this huge ice-floe to the height of fifteen metres (forty-five feet). When spring finally came and the ice began to melt, icebergs floated down the Bosporos, blocking the entrance to the Sea of Marmara and filling the Golden Horn. Part of the quay was damaged by a particularly large iceberg, which, although it must have grounded and broken into three pieces, was still higher than the sea-walls of the city.

Tekfur Sarayi, Istanbul. Although now little more than a shell, this palace close to the walls of Constantinople gives us a fascinating glimpse of later secular building in the city. It probably dates from the early fourteenth century, and its facade of patterned bricks and rounded windows suggests that its builders may have had some experience of earlier Italian architecture.

Another way in which the city changed markedly was in the arrival of colonies of foreign traders. There had, from the early centuries, always been a Latin quarter in Constantinople, where Italians lived, and where services were held which followed the Roman Catholic form of the liturgy. The Venetians, always the most persistent and skilful traders, were particularly successful in creating excellent conditions for themselves. Under a charter of 1082 they were allowed, in return for political help from their fleet, to trade freely all over the Byzantine Empire without payment of any dues and without inspection by the Byzantine customs; in Constantinople itself, the Venetians were given a large quarter, with many shops and warehouses. In time the Genoese built up a considerable colony in Pera, on the far side of the Golden Horn from the main city; there they were even allowed in the thirteenth century to build their own defensive walls, and they were governed by their own *podestà*, appointed direct from Genoa. While these were the two most important commercial groups of foreigners, there were many others represented in Constantinople: Pisans, Florentines, Sicilians, merchants from the Adriatic cities such as Ancona and Ragusa, traders from Provence and Catalonia — all could have been found bargaining on the quays of the Golden Horn, and walking in the streets and squares of the city. It is important to realize how cosmopolitan a place it always was.

Yet, paradoxically, it was partly the wealth that these foreign merchants brought to the city, and their very clear display of it that caused the city's greatest disaster ever to take place until its final capture by the Turks. This was the episode of 1204, when the Fourth Crusade, supposedly on its way to the Holy Land, was diverted and its forces used to enter and sack Constantinople. In this truly disgraceful affair, of which the minor details are still debated, the most obvious factor was the naked greed of the Western powers for the untold wealth that was to be found within the walls of the city.

Politically, the most important result of this catastrophe was that the Byzantine Emperor was deposed, and a Western usurper, Baldwin of Flanders, was placed on the throne of the Caesars. There was to be a succession of these Latin emperors until 1261, when Michael VIII, of the Palaeologue dynasty, finally recovered the throne for the Byzantines. Economically, this period of Latin rule depleted the resources of the Empire to such an extent that it never fully recovered. While there were later revivals of art and learning, the underlying wealth on which so much of the Byzantine achievement had been based was gone forever. Artistically, the events of 1204 were in some ways the least disastrous aspect of the Fourth Crusade. While the Latin emperors ruled in Constantinople, the Byzantines withdrew to Nicaea on the mainland of Asia Minor, and there set up a small court which perpetuated their great traditions in the arts and in learning. Modern scholarship is only now coming to a realization of the achievements of the exiled dynasty, with its limited resources and its dreams of one day returning home. But for Western Europe the most important outcome of the sacking of Constantinople in the field of the arts was the arrival in the West of enormous quantities of Byzantine artefacts. The result of the pillage of 1204, and the subsequent years of looting and theft, was that literally thousands of Byzantine works of art in the form of gold and silver reliquaries, ornaments and vessels of all kinds, illuminated manuscripts, sculptures, textiles and ivories flooded into the West, where many can still be seen in the treasuries of French, Italian and German cathedrals. The Sainte Chapelle in Paris was actually built to house all the relics that were looted in 1204, and the treasury of St Mark's in Venice is also mainly filled with crusaders' booty. Ironically, this means that people now can enjoy much of Byzantine art that would otherwise have been lost forever; for since the crusaders in their greed carried off these works as prizes, and therefore kept many of them in safety, the centuries of Turkish neglect and destruction that followed the capture of the city in 1453 would doubtless have produced a greater eventual loss. Christian rapacity may have saved much that Islam, with its traditional antipathy to figural art, would have eventually destroyed, either through religious zeal or passive neglect.

In view of the general debility of the Empire after the return of Michael VIII to Constantinople, it is astonishing what superlative works of art and architecture the city produced. In literature and learning, too, this period was supremely accomplished. It is almost as though the Byzantines saw their last two centuries as an Indian Summer, in which the last flowering of their brilliant genius could take place. For they must have seen the writing on the wall. Inexorably, the Turkish grip was tightening. In 1308 the Ottoman army entered Europe; in 1329 Nicaea was captured, and in 1357 Adrianople; in 1373 the Emperor John V Palaeologus became the vassal of the Ottoman Sultan Murad. In his desperation to win support from the West, John V travelled to Rome in 1369 and publicly adopted the Roman faith, reading his confession aloud in St Peter's, and acknowledging the Pope to be the head of all Christians. But this was to get him nowhere. Not only did the Byzantine people completely reject any thought of union, but the Emperor, on his way back to Constantinople through Venice, was arrested as a debtor, and had to be redeemed by his son.

With the Empire in such a reduced condition, it is amazing that a few Byzantine patrons were still able to carry out expensive projects of restoration and embellishment, have manuscripts illuminated and icons painted. What has been called the Palaeologue Renaissance took place, and it shows that there were still artists in the city capable of reviving the glories of the earlier centuries; with their capacity for ceaseless renewal, they created a new style of effortless variety, still completely Byzantine but with its own character of decorative, fluid grace. One important patron was Theodore Metochites (1270—1332). A scholar with an extensive library, a man of letters, and a diplomat who arranged some important political marriages, he became eventually the Grand Vizier, or Prime Minister of the whole Empire; at this time (in 1321) he was also given the title of Grand Logothete

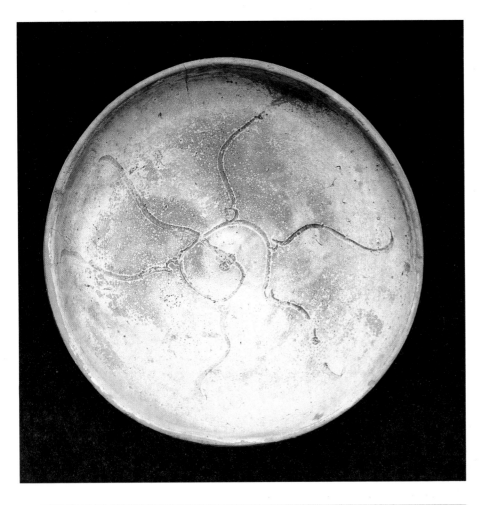

Above: twelfth-century pottery redware bowl with abstract design.
Below: twelfth-century pottery redware bowl with bird decoration. Pottery plates and bowls must have been used principally by the poorer citizens, and so their decoration and glazes have a directness and charm close to peasant art. Both these bowls have incised underglaze decoration, with the design scored into the soft clay, pressing through a layer of white 'slip' before the final glazing and firing.

60

of the Treasury. A fascinating character, very typical of the later Byzantine tradition of 'mandarin civil servant', Metochites left one of the outstanding examples of Palaeologue church decoration behind when he died. Between about 1316 and 1321 he rebuilt and added to the Church of St Saviour in Chora (which had already been restored by Justinian and rebuilt under Alexius I).

By one of those happy miracles of history, this church has survived. Although damaged in some areas, most of its interior is now to be seen as it was in the 1320s when Metochites attended the services there with his monks. Used for centuries as a mosque, and still usually called the Kariye Djami, its frescoes and mosaics were plastered and whitewashed. In this way most of the decoration was protected from the depredations of Islam, while simple good fortune has kept it largely undisturbed by earthquake or fire. To enter this building is to walk into the world of late Byzantium at its rich and brilliant height. The posturing, elegant figures with their fluttering draperies stand out from the glittering gold background of the mosaics on walls, niches and ribbed cupolas; in the chapel which Metochites added to the church, the dynamism of the frescoed scenes, dominated by the *Last Judgement* and the frighteningly powerful *Anastasis*, convey the astonishing energy of the last phase of Byzantine artistic life.

For this, and a few other late projects of this kind, must have been exceptional. It is probable that only a few favoured officials could afford to finance works on this scale, while the Emperor's resources were strained to breaking point in his efforts to protect the city, and what was left of the Empire, from the Turkish menace. Surely a truer picture of the city in the evening of its days is found in the descriptions of travellers who visited it in the fourteenth and early fifteenth centuries. A Spaniard, Ruy Gonzales de Clavijo, who was in Constantinople in 1403 wrote: 'Everywhere throughout the city there are many great palaces, churches and monasteries, but most of them are now in ruins. It is very evident, though, that in former days when Constantinople was in its prime it was one of the noblest capitals of the whole world.' A further touch is added by an Arab geographer, writing during the lifetime of Metochites; he commented that 'Within the city there are sown fields and gardens, and there are many ruined houses.' But perhaps the most telling and pathetic account from these twilight years of Byzantium is that of the wedding feast of the Emperor John V in the mid-fourteenth century, given by the historian Nicephorus Gregoras. By then all the imperial treasures had been sold, no funds remained in the Emperor's coffers, and taxes owed from the few remaining provinces were unpaid and could not be collected:

> At that time the palace was so poor that there was no cup or goblet of gold or silver; some were of pewter and the rest of pottery . . . and at the festivities most of the imperial diadems and regalia only appeared to be of gold and jewels; in reality they were of leather, and were only gilded, as tanners do sometimes, or were made of glass which reflected in different colours. Just occasionally, here and there, precious stones could be seen which have a genuine sparkle, and the lustre of real pearls, which do not deceive the eye. To such a degree the ancient wealth and brilliance of the Roman Empire had fallen, entirely gone out and perished, so that it is not without shame that I tell this story.

So the last centuries of Byzantium saw Constantinople, the city which was heir to the Caesars, encircled by the Ottoman forces, its buildings falling into ruin, and even the Emperor drinking from pewter and pottery; in only a few corners of the city did the ancient light of learning and culture still flicker among the crumbling palaces and churches.

As part of the great revival in the arts that took place under the Paleologue dynasty, a large mosaic was installed in the South Gallery of Hagia Sophia. This detail of the enthroned Christ conveys the brilliance and maturity of this last phase of Byzantine art in Constantinople. Even the gold background to the figures has been patterned to reflect and scatter the light as it falls across the surface of the mosaic tesserae.

THE BYZANTINE ARMY AND NAVY

Throughout its history Byzantium was beset by foreign powers, all of which coveted the territory to which it was easiest for them to lay claim. Huns, Slavs, Magyars, Saracens, Turks — all were enemies of the Byzantines at one time or another. The Byzantine mentality was not, in fact, aggressive. Had the Empire, as it existed in the fourth century, been left to itself, without incursions and annexations by tribes on its borders, it is hard to envisage any natural process of territorial expansion taking place. Unlike the Moslems, whose commitment was to constant conquest of new lands, the Byzantines were for most of their existence naturally much more on the defensive.

Despite the fact that much of the population of Constantinople came from coastal areas of the Mediterranean, which had a strong tradition of sea travel, it was always the Army that was the senior service. Initially this must have been due to the Byzantines' Roman inheritance, but as the centuries passed it became clear that the survival of the Byzantines depended most heavily on their ability to fight successfully on land. The pre-eminence of the Army was also embedded in the system of government; for example, the Army was one of the three bodies that acclaimed a new emperor — the Navy had no such voice in official state practice. Even the Byzantine civil service was organized to some extent along military lines; civil servants wore a form of dress that could almost be called a uniform, and their 'badge of office' was a rather military looking belt. Indeed, entering the civil service was called 'taking the belt'.

Given the substantially military character of official life and the undisputed need for an effective army, it is perhaps surprising that soldiers were not more evident in the day-to-day life of Constantinople. In the streets and squares of the city it would have been far more common to see merchants, tradesmen, shopkeepers, civil officials of various kinds, monks and priests than soldiers in any large numbers. This was due to several factors. The Byzantine genius for organization meant that the Empire could be defended with a surprisingly small standing army. The figure of 120,000 is usually given as the maximum number that the Byzantine Army reached, and for much of the time it was less than this. More important still, in this context, was that the Army was organized on the system known as 'themes'. This was an essentially defensive concept of the use of the army, that had been largely established by the eighth century. It involved the division of the Empire into areas, and the stationing of regiments of troops in each area with responsibility for its defence. These regiments were called themes. The commander of the regiment was also the civil governor of the district, and was therefore a figure of considerable importance. As the frontiers were extended or contracted, new themes were created or old ones amalgamated. Besides giving a fundamentally military character to the way the Empire was organized, this system meant that a greater part of the Army was dispersed, and only a relatively small number of troops would have been found in Constantinople itself at any one time.

At all times there had been a force of élite troops whose sole duty was to guard the person of the emperor. This palace guard was an inheritance from the Caesars, but it would have been necessary in any case. Its title and composition changed during the centuries, but these were the soldiers that were most in evidence in Constantinople itself. They had a distinctive uniform, and there was a long-standing tradition that this imperial bodyguard was to be made up of foreign troops. The famous Varangian Guard that was established by the eleventh century contained only foreigners: Germans, English, Franks, Russians, even Vikings all served in it. It was presumably the loyalty due to the ultimate power of the emperor, who paid them generously, that made them more reliable than any body of local troops, which might have been attracted to an internal usurper.

The Byzantine Army inevitably reflected the diversity of races that made up the Empire, with the varying skills of different tribes all being put to the service of the state. The cavalry, for example, tended to come from the hinterland of Asia Minor, where the local population had a long tradition of brilliant horsemanship. After the imperial guard, the cavalry was the supreme fighting force of the Army. Again and again, it was the waves of armed riders, some shooting arrows from the saddle, others more heavily armed with lances, that turned the tide of a battle, often fighting against much more numerous troops. The cavalry were armed with iron helmets, chain-mail or scale armour shirts, shields and metal breastplates, and had swords and daggers as hand weapons, with lances or bows and arrows. They were fully professional, and highly paid, although they needed considerable support from civilian camp-followers. It was this concentration on the use of expert professionals that allowed the Byzantines to survive with relatively small regular forces.

Foot-soldiers had originally been the mainstay of the Roman army, but by the fourth and fifth centuries they had become no match for the barbarians on horseback; it was from this quite early stage that the Byzantine cavalry was built up. The foot-soldiers still had a number of vital functions, however, particularly when fighting battles with other forces also on foot, such as the Slavs and Franks. They would also have come into their own in terrain where the cavalry did not have sufficient room to manoeuvre, as in the rocky mountainous country, with steep gorges and defiles. They were more heavily armed than the cavalry, having, besides the usual armour, larger shields, maces, broadswords, bows and arrows and javelins. Every soldier's shield was coloured to identify him with his particular regiment.

It is clear from the few military handbooks that have survived that the Byzantine Army was never known for rash and daredevil fighting actions. Caution was their watchword. All leaders, from generals down, were to be on the look-out for surprise attacks; they should never take their men into a position where they could be ambushed, or leave their flanks unguarded. Indeed, where possible they should undermine the enemy's morale to the point where a pitched battle might be avoided; this could be done, for instance, by such devious ploys as sending a compromising letter to an enemy general, and ensuring that it was intercepted by one of his lesser commanders. If it was important to gain time — and this could often be the case, while reinforcements from neighbouring themes were given a chance to come to the scene — a general might open a lengthy negotiation of terms for a truce to which he had no intention of agreeing once his forces had been increased.

64

This scene from the historical Chronicle of John Scylitzes (fol. 43. v.), c. 1300, gives
a clear idea of the military aspect of an emperor's rule, even when he was still
within the city. Here the Emperor Theophilus is seen with his bodyguard in the streets
of the city, just outside the Church of Blachernae. He is dispensing justice to
a widow who approaches him with some complaint, while two priests look on from the
doorway of the church.

The Byzantines always used their forces with the greatest good sense and intelligence, wherever they could matching their strength to the enemy's weakness. If it was to their advantage, they paid tribute to a threatening invader, buying him off with gold rather than risking a battle on the wrong terms. It was probably in 924 that the citizens of Constantinople witnessed just such a negotiation; the greatest of the Bulgarian leaders, Simeon, came to parley with the Emperor, Romanus Lecapenus, under the very walls of Constantinople. The Emperor reached the scene first, arriving in the imperial yacht which had probably been sailed round from the Boucleon harbour below the Great Palace, while Simeon arrived from the landward side. With great ceremony the discussions were opened — Romanus's opening speech has been preserved — and eventually a figure was agreed upon that Simeon should be paid annually, provided he left the city alone. While not strictly military, negotiations like these were an outcome of the Byzantine approach to military strategy.

This was also the case with their Navy. There had been no great naval

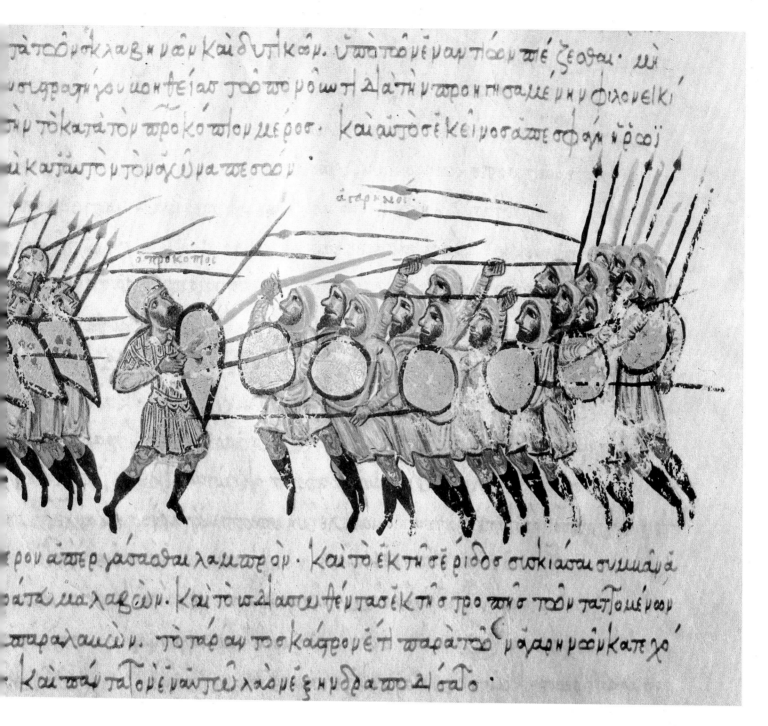

Above left: This illustration from the Chronicle of John Scylitzes (fol. 217 r.) shows an event from military history. The Bulgars are besieging Thessaloniki, and their leader, Deleanos, receives another of the Bulgar leaders in his tent. The tented camp of the Bulgar army can be seen in the background.

Below left: The different styles of fighting and armament of the Byzantines and Seljuks can be seen in this miniature from the same chronicle (fol. 234. r.). Byzantine cavalrymen tended to rely largely on the use of their lances, and rode without stirrups, while the Seljuks had lances and bows and arrows; as they had stirrups they could shoot from the saddle with considerable accuracy.

Above: In this miniature (fol. 99. v.) the foot soldiers of Emperor Basil I, distinguished by their longer shields, desert their general in the face of the hostile Arab forces, who carry round shields. The Byzantine general, called Procopius, is killed. Byzantine military leaders often relied more on diplomacy or cunning, avoiding pitched battles where possible.

ρελατα οτα τε· και του δ ιω τοορ δκι τα και ατα λι σα οιο· τρε ω ωτ τοι ιου λγατοοι· αιιοδ ω ωσ
προσ κ ινουν τι α λκι νη σι ηωοι λι ιστ ερ τι· το υ μαρτυρ ος α ρονι ου ε ιν ου ι τι θ ομα ικι τ
ρα τ η καν τα τρι ν α νι σω αλι Ζου τος· και νι ετι ιμν ιι ς ου

Above left: This miniature from the Chronicle of John Scylitzes (fol. 217. r.) is of an episode of the siege of Thessaloniki by the Bulgars. The Byzantine forces are making a sortie from the gates of the city, and putting the Bulgar horsemen to flight. Trumpeters on the walls sound the signal for the attack.

Below left: This miniature (fol. 217. v.) shows the final defeat of the Bulgars by the Emperor Michael IV the Paphlagonian, who is seated alone on his throne. The Bulgars put up a wooden palisade near Prilep, which is seen here between the two groups of soldiers, but the Byzantine forces broke it down.

inheritance from ancient Rome — the Mediterranean had been just a large Roman lake, with no enemies of sufficient significance on it to justify maintaining anything like a proper fleet. In the early centuries of Byzantium the main threats to the empire came from the land rather than the sea, but the expansion of the Arabs changed this trend, and from the seventh century onwards there was always need for a Byzantine fleet.

The Navy was in fact only established officially when the themes were founded; in the same way that a general was in charge of a given area, so the two naval themes that were set up were each under the control of an admiral. One of them, the Cibyrrhaeot theme, covered the southern coasts of Asia Minor, while the other, the Aegean theme, was allocated the islands of the Aegean that were under Byzantine control. This one became very powerful, and it may have been because the emperors of the Isaurian dynasty were predominantly soldiers that they felt it to be too much of

Above right: This miniature (fol. 42. v.) shows the Emperor Theophilus making a proclamation from the throne. He is flanked by his bodyguard, who are bare-headed, while the different ranks of the court officials on either side are distinguished by the various kinds of headgear they wear.

Below right: Although the artist has had to compress the miniature seen here (fol. 222. r.) he has attempted to depict a Byzantine dromond — in this case with three banks of oars. A court official is embarking on it, and the rowers are seated at their benches.

a threat to their safety, and began to reduce its influence in the later eighth century. Before that, however, the Aegean theme had twice driven off attacks on Constantinople by Arab fleets, and it might have changed the shape of Byzantine history even further had there been later both the resources and the intention to support it fully. By the eleventh and twelfth centuries, in spite of periods of great usefulness, the Navy was in almost permanent decline; it was only during the period of the Nicaean emperors in the thirteenth century that it returned to some favour, as they must have seen it as one of the tools for eventually ousting the Frankish rulers in Constantinople.

The usual form of a Byzantine naval vessel was that of a galley, usually with two banks of oars; it was called a *dromond*, or 'runner'. There were at least two different types, one being larger and the other being capable of faster travel, and having greater manoeuvrability. In times of need, merchant ships could be commandeered. There may never have been more than about 200 ships regularly in use, and often there were fewer than 100.

As with the use of land forces, it was the inventive intelligence of the Byzantines that allowed them to survive in a sea-faring area of the world with many hostile neighbours, but with such relatively modest naval strength. One particular form that this inventiveness took was a weapon which struck fear throughout the medieval world. It was called 'Greek fire', and the process for making it was a closely guarded secret for centuries. A highly combustible chemical fluid which ignited under any sort of impact, it seems to have been invented by a Greek-Syrian architect called Callinicus some time in the seventh century. It was a combination of various chemicals such as naphtha and saltpetre, and it could be used either encased in clay containers, which were thrown or catapulted and which exploded on hitting the target, or it could be squirted through tubes under pressure. In either case its effects were devastating, as it not only set fire to any ships that it landed on, but could even burn on the surface of the water. Again and again it was Greek fire that was the decisive factor in Byzantine sea battles, its effects being even more terrifying as it could be directed sideways or even downwards. Here is how Princess Anna Comnena described the Emperor Alexius' preparation of ships with Greek fire for use against the Pisans:

> As the Emperor knew that the Pisans were skilled in sea warfare, and was apprehensive about having a battle with them, on the prow of each ship that he had had built he had a head fixed of a lion, or other land-animal, open-mouthed, made in bronze or iron and gilded all over, so that just the sight of them was terrifying. And the fire that was to be directed against the enemy through tubes he made to pass through the mouths of the beasts, so that it looked as if they were vomiting fire.

It is unlikely that the Princess herself would have seen these ships in action, but even the sight of them as they were being built under her father's supervision in the dockyards of Constantinople was enough for her to be able to envisage their effect on the enemy. Just as the throne-room of the palace was designed to create an overwhelming impression on any visiting diplomat, so the 'secret weapon' of Greek fire — terrifying enough at any time — was funnelled out of the gilded heads of open-mouthed beasts.

This deadly fluid could also be used on land. While it was too dangerous to be carried any distance on military campaigns, as it could ignite so easily, it certainly was used when the city was under siege. It could be squirted from the walls on to wooden siege towers that the enemy brought up, and was most often used in defensive fighting of this kind. Greek fire finally fell into disuse when it was superseded by gunpowder and cannon in the fourteenth century, and there is no mention of its use in the last defence of Constantinople in 1453.

CITY LIFE
AND TRADE

Silver hyperper of Manuel II (1391–1425), reverse. The entire history of the Byzantine state could be written from its coinage, displaying, as it does, all the complex changes in the Empire, and its economy over more than eleven centuries. The hyperper was introduced in a reform of the currency made by Alexius I in 1092; as with the solidus, the basic measure concerned the weight of the metal used. Byzantine coins in silver are considerably rarer than those in gold, and tend to be concentrated in the later periods of the Empire's existence. That of Manuel II displays the great deterioration in style and technique that mirrors the fortunes of the city and its economy.

While to later centuries the achievements of the Byzantines in the field of the arts and learning have been most evident, it should not be forgotten that they were also one of the great trading nations of the world. Their tremendous cultural achievements were built on a fundamental economic strength — indeed they would not have been possible without it. And this strength was founded on the commercial expertise of the huge merchant population of Constantinople. The decline of Byzantium is closely linked to its diminishing opportunities in trade; the highly profitable overland trade routes to the Far East were lost when the Seljuks took control of most of Asia Minor in the eleventh century, and the crusaders did further economic damage in the following century. As it became possible for goods to be exported to the West from Syrian ports, avoiding harbour dues in Constantinople, so the city's commercial decline was accelerated.

So, when speaking of the day to day life of Constantinople in the centuries of its greatness, it is necessary to envisage the constant traffic of goods through the city, both from overland and on the quays of the Golden Horn. In a sense this was the life-blood of the Empire, without which little else could have been achieved. This emphasis on world trade, with the city at the meeting point of East and West, naturally encouraged a large population of foreign merchants. These tended to be mostly from Western Europe, and by about 1180 there were some 60,000 of them living in the city. This was a very noticeable proportion of the entire population. In the markets, shops and streets of the city it was usual to see foreigners moving among the local city-dwellers — Genoese, Provençals, Catalans, Amalfitans, Venetians — and all would have been distinguishable by the variety of clothing they wore.

This vigorous commercial life was, like everything else in Byzantium, very carefully controlled by a highly developed bureaucracy. Foreign traders had to report on arrival to the eparch, or prefect, of Constantinople. They were only allowed to stay for three months, and the small army of civil servants that the eparch employed kept a strict check on all the transactions that were carried out by all these thousands of foreign merchants. Every item exported or imported was subject to a tax of ten per cent; for exports this was collected in the city itself, and for incoming goods it was levied on the routes into the city, either further up the Bosporos or, for cargoes coming from the West, on the Dardanelles.

Control was also extended to all aspects of the very vigorous manufacturing life of the city. By great good fortune a manuscript has survived from the tenth century called the *Book of the Eparch*. It is a kind of handbook of the regulations by which the Eparch and his many officials governed the

Above: The relief carvings on the base of the Egyptian obelisk that the Emperor Theodosius had erected in the hippodrome at Constantinople show the great importance that was attached to the events that took place there. The hippodrome was the natural focus of most of the secular life of the city, and the presence of the Emperor would have been obligatory. A special 'royal box' was built for him and the Empress, which could be entered directly from the Great Palace.

Below: Gold scyphate (coin) of Romanus IV (1067–1071), obverse. The scyphate (the word means 'cup shaped'), seen here shows Romanus IV and his wife Eudocia being blessed by Christ. This official display of the divine nature of the emperor's rule was one of the commonest themes on Byzantine coinage.

practice of all the various trades and professions in the city. It is divided into twenty-two chapters, each dealing with a different group, or profession; they include notaries, bankers and moneychangers, merchants of raw silk, raw silk dressers, silk-dyers, perfumiers, saddlers, butchers, pork-butchers, innkeepers, bakers and so on. Each group was rigorously compartmentalized, and no one was allowed to move from one trade to another without permission. The range of penalties and punishments available to the eparch for enforcing the regulations was considerable, although the most extreme were reserved for offences concerning abuse of currency.

To illustrate the extent of the control under which everyone in the city worked, here are a few of the injuctions found in the *Book of the Eparch:*
— No silversmith was allowed to work at home, but only in the workshops on the Mese (thus the eparch's inspectors could keep a closer eye on what the silversmith was doing).
— Silk of a particular large size and purple colour could only be bought for use by the emperor (this regulation was broken by Liutprand of Cremona when he visited the city in 949, and the silk he had bought to take home was confiscated by the Byzantine customs).
— No innkeeper was allowed to sell drink in vessels which did not bear the official stamp giving the correct measure; if he did, and was caught, he could be flogged, shaved and expelled from the guild.
— If a money-changer was offered a piece of false money, he had to take it, with the man who had offered it, to the eparch; if he was ever found not to have done this, he also could be flogged, shaved and expelled from the money-changer's guild.
— Whoever 'takes it upon himself to sell silver to be manufactured and sold shall have his hand cut off.' This is the most severe punishment mentioned in the *Book of the Eparch,* and it is confined to this offence; it must relate to the possible practice of melting down coinage to be made into silver, and so illustrates the seriousness with which the Byzantines regarded the maintenance of the value of their currency.

The Byzantine gold *nomisma,* known to all Europe and beyond as the *bezant,* was, in effect, the only international currency. It was therefore essential that its purity be beyond question (though the later emperors were to fight a losing battle to preserve its value).

In the same way that all trades were centrally controlled by the eparch, so he fixed the prices of many of the goods, or delegated the task to the heads of particular guilds. In particular, he regulated the exchange rates offered by the money-changers. The Byzantine civilization was also the first to introduce the practice of stamping silver products to show that they had been assayed, and were of the correct degree of purity. As one of the stamps used was a portrait of the reigning emperor, Byzantine silver can be dated much more accurately today than can most medieval works of this kind. Their reason for this care, besides their interest in maintaining records of the wealth that the city produced, must also have related to the general financial stability of the state, as silver would have commonly been used as surety for raising loans.

Just how seriously the Byzantines took the regulation of the commercial side of city life is shown by the comment of the Spanish traveller, Ruy de Clavijo, writing within fifty years of the fall of the city:

> In a street ... stand the Stocks, firmly built on the ground, where are set those convicted of heinous crime, and about to be imprisoned; or those who have contravened the laws and ordinances of the city authorities, namely, for instance, those who sell bread and meat with false weight. All such are exposed in the Stocks, where they remain night and day at the mercy of the rain and wind, none being allowed to succour them.

The gold solidus, of which an example from the reign of Heraclius is seen here, was the basic gold coin struck from the time of Constantine onwards. Originally, seventy-two were struck from one pound of pure gold. This one must date from between 632 and the year of Heraclius' death, 641, as his son, who was given the title of Caesar, is included.

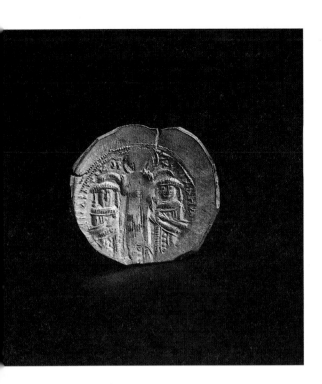

The gold hyperper of Andronicus II, minted between 1295 and 1320, conveys the concept of the divinely ordained rule of the Emperor, who is seen, with his son Michael IX, kneeling beside Christ, who blesses them both.

It is no surprise, in view of the highly organized way that the commercial life of Constantinople was governed, to find that there was also a strong basic framework of civic authority. Any urban society as large and complex as this would always have needed some kind of structure for maintaining the needs of city life. From the early centuries of the city's existence — quite when is not known — the people of Constantinople had been divided into four bodies known as 'demes', which were comparable in function to the 'wards' of a modern British city. These were named after four colours — blue, green, white and red; while this colour scheme may originally have provided a further link with ancient Rome, where these colours were used to identify rival groups who attended the chariot races in the Circus, its adoption in the newly founded city may have had wider implications. The original purpose of the demes was that they should be self-governing municipal bodies concerned with providing the basic services and necessities for the life of the city, and assisting in communal tasks such as the building of roads and defences.

It is not clear when these began to change their function and identity, merging into two more basic groups. For instance, when it was decreed that new land walls of the city had to be built in 410, the organization of the labour was assigned to the Greens and the Blues. All the population had to assist, either by contributing money or by working on the construction, but the way that the prefect was able to accomplish this huge project was by using the basic organization provided by these two demes. Then at an early stage it seems that the Whites became merged with the Blues and the Reds with the Greens, and their civic functions were simplified; under an official called a *demarch*, the Blues seem to have been responsible for the city's roads and other amenities, and for taking precautions against fires, while the Greens acted as a part-time garrison, having a more military function.

These two demes became extremely powerful, and formed the focus for much of the popular feeling of the citizens. They were the nearest organ that the Byzantines achieved for expressing the will of the people. During the later fifth and sixth centuries they were so powerful that they had to be taken into consideration at the highest level; most of the time emperors could play one faction off against the other, but when popular feeling ran sufficiently high the Blues and Greens could combine with devastating effect. The most famous such occasion was in 532, when the high taxes levied by Justinian to finance his military campaigns eventually sparked off the so-called Nika riots, which ended with the burning down of the church of Hagia Sofia. It was only the dominant will-power of the Empress Theodora that prevented Justinian from abdicating in the face of this expression of united popular fury. As the centuries passed the demes lost their political power, but still played a part in the ceremonial life of the court. It was as representatives of the people that they filled a role in the services of the Great Church; in the tenth century *Book of Ceremonies*, the Blues and Greens both have specified acclamations with which they greet the emperor or empress at coronations, at Christmas and Easter services, and on other occasions.

But above all, the Blues and Greens were identified with the life of the circus. If they had a 'home', that was it. The races in the hippodrome provided the clearest link with the heritage of ancient Rome, and it was there that the people gave vent to their emotions as they encouraged their favourite riders. Entry to the circus was free, and on race days there were sessions both in the morning and in the afternoon. Four chariots would race at a time, and each race would be of seven laps — a distance of about three kilometres (one and a half miles). They were savagely contested, with rough riding producing many accidents, and some fatalities. The

Above, right and left: Six-sided silver vessel, with busts of Christ and saints, 602—610. Found in Cyprus at the end of the last century, probably a censer. The base is marked by control stamps.

Below: Byzantine interest in trade is conveyed by the large numbers of weights that have survived, and the importance given to them is emphasized by the fine decoration they often bear. The diameter of the largest weight is 27.7 mm, and the smallest measures 11.1 by 10.5 mm.

prestige of the circus champions was enormous; the most successful became immensely wealthy and had statues of themselves erected in the vicinity of the hippodrome. Besides receiving a prize of money, the winner of each race was presented with a cloak and a wreath. He climbed the steps of the emperor's box to receive these from the emperor's hands, accompanied by the leader of the faction that had supported him. The factions were separated, with the Greens sitting to the left of the emperor, and the Blues to the right.

While the commercial life of the city, with the amusements of the circus and the processions and other ceremonies in the area of Hagia Sophia and the Great Palace, would have represented the more public side of Byzantine life, there were many other activities and institutions that, though less in evidence, contributed enormously to the character of Constantinople.

The whole apparatus of education and learning — schools or their equivalent, university life, the production and sale of books — was immensely important to Byzantine culture, but was by its nature far more private. Under Constantine and the early emperors, education was seen as a state responsibility. A school had been founded by Constantine as part of the inauguration of his city, and it was to survive until the sixth century in successive locations; it seems to have finally disappeared under Justinian, who is known to have closed the school at Athens. From that time, all of what is now called primary and secondary education would have been available only from private tutors, or from ecclesiastics teaching in churches or monasteries; there was a school, for instance, at the Church of the Apostles in the eleventh century, and there were others attached to the Studion Monastery and other church foundations. These would have taught the liberal arts, which formed the basic education of the Middle Ages, starting with grammar at the age of about six (including, of course, reading and writing as well as grammar itself). Practice in reading would have been given only through works by the classical authors, particularly Homer, commentaries on these works, and the Bible. At fourteen or so the pupil would progress to rhetoric with the study of pronunciation, and its application in the works of Greek authors such as Demosthenes. This would be followed by philosophy, and then by the other arts of arithmetic, geometry, astronomy and music.

*Above right and left: This flat, silver plate
with niello decoration was found in the same
hoard in Cyprus as the silver vessel on
page 76.* *Dating from between 578 and 582,
it was in all likelihood used as a paten,
holding the bread at the liturgy. The fact that
one of the stamps on the base of these objects
is very often a portrait of the emperor of
the time is why it is possible to be so certain
about their dates. The use of these stamps
is an indication of the extent to which the
Byzantines developed systems for controlling
all the commercial life of the city.*

The transition to 'higher education' would have been far less clear-cut
than it is now; indeed the original university of Constantinople had gradually
diminished in importance, until it finally disappeared in the seventh century.
It should be remembered that during the early centuries the city was
a new arrival, struggling for acceptance among the far more ancient centres
of Mediterranean learning such as Alexandria, Athens, Antioch and Beirut.
So a citizen who wanted to further his studies to become a lawyer or a doctor,
or to enter the Civil Service, would have had to learn mostly from ecclesiastics. As the centuries passed the old fear of paganism which still attached
to learning and university study dwindled, and secular learning revived
correspondingly. In the ninth century the university was started again, but
it had opponents in the church hierarchy, and again disappeared. In its
final form it was a Law School, initiated by Constantine IX in the eleventh
century, and thus it survived until the Fourth Crusade in 1204.

One constant factor was the great admiration that the Byzantines always
had for education and learning in any form. A good education was certainly
the key to advancement in almost any field, but the financial aspects of
obtaining one must often have been formidable. Just consider the difficulty
and expense of producing one book. Sufficient parchment first had to be
obtained; this would probably come from the skins of sheep or goats, and
so was to some extent seasonal — supplies were often short by December or
January. A medium-sized book of 200 pages might take the skins of about
twenty sheep, and these had to be tanned and scraped by hand. After
being cut and folded they were taken to a copyist. He ruled the lines on
each page, and copied the work that was wanted with a quill pen and ink.
All these processes, followed by that of binding, must have taken hundreds
of man-hours. It is impossible to give meaningful translations of medieval
prices into modern equivalents, but one medium-sized book probably

Above: This scene from the early fourteenth-century mosaics in the Kariye Djami shows a scene that any Byzantine would have understood well: the Holy Family being enrolled for taxation by their Roman rulers. All aspects of life in Constantinople were controlled by a well-organized bureaucracy, and the mosaicist here has taken evident pleasure in showing the details of a process that his patron would have known intimately.

Below: Miniature from an eleventh-century manuscript of the Cynegetica of the Pseudo-Oppian, cod. gr. 479. fol. 59. r. This scene of three men fishing must be regarded as happening at night, as there is a light fixed over the stern. The artist has been careful to show the exact workings of the nets that were then in use. Fish would have formed a valuable part of the Byzantine domestic economy in coastal areas.

represented for a Byzantine scholar the same sort of investment that a small car would for his modern counterpart. For more elaborate or larger books, involving decorated headpieces to the chapters, and some illustrations, the cost would be multiplied several times. This suggests that there must have been some sort of second-hand trade, but again, books would have kept their value even for centuries, and so could never have been cheap. The main subject-matter of Byzantine libraries — the classics, the Bible, theological writings from the early Church Fathers — never went out of date; only the physical decay of books would have caused their replacement.

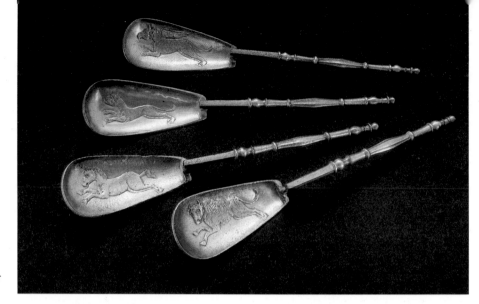

Above right: These four silver spoons from a set of eleven that was found in Cyprus, were clearly for secular use, with finely worked animal decoration in the bowls. They probably date from about 600, and may have been buried just before the Arabs attacked Cyprus in 653—54. The palaces of the rich would have contained countless examples of such work.

Below right: These arm-bands are each made from two hinged pieces of gold, with brilliantly coloured cloisonné enamels set in panels all round. Such arm-bands formed part of Byzantine court dress, and so would have been worn with richly coloured robes. These probably date from the ninth or tenth century.

Below: In this relief from the base of the Obelisk of Theodosius, the Emperor and his family are standing to award the laurel wreath to the victor of the races.

Personal jewellery such as these finger-rings would have been produced in large quantities in the workshops of Constantinople.
In some cases the decoration has a secular theme, or is of an abstract character, but the existence of many items of jewellery decorated with religious subject-matter indicates how interwoven these two aspects of life had become.

From these general considerations it is clear that any advanced education could have been available only to a fortunate few. The expense of paying tutors and assembling a small working library must always have been substantial. Yet it was possible for the son of quite poor parents, if he were clever and industrious, to reach the highest offices of the state. An example of just such a man was Theodore Metochites, the restorer of the Monastery of the Chora (the Kariye Djami). The son of disgraced and banished parents, he worked his way up the ladder of the Byzantine civil service, ending as Prime Minister of the Empire and Grand Logothete of the Treasury. He never abandoned his intellectual pursuits, writing poems, essays, commentaries on Aristotle and an introduction to astronomy; these were the activities of his leisure hours. He can be pictured as a typical senior civil servant of his age, spending his days fulfilling his state duties, and in close touch with the Emperor, and at night returning to his study to read and write. The wealth that he accumulated in his office from the sale of favours and sinecures he later spent on the restoration of the monastery he had adopted. He enjoyed attending the night services there with the monks, and at the very end of his life he actually became a monk. Even this was probably not unusual, as it was in keeping with the more unworldly, spiritual side of Byzantine life.

But for the less fortunate citizens life had pleasures and compensations of a different sort. Besides free admission to the circus, there was a basic form of welfare state, with one of the imperial departments of state being responsible for orphanages and homes for the aged. Care for the sick fell largely to the monasteries and convents, a number of which had hospitals attached to them. These displayed the more practical side of the Byzantine character. For example, the large monastery of St Saviour Pantocrator had a hospital that was endowed by John II Comnenus in the twelfth century. It had five wards, with ten beds in each ward; surgical cases were kept separate from medical cases, and of course women patients were separated from men. There were eleven doctors to service it, one of whom was a woman, a number of other assistants, and a medical professor to instruct new doctors. The study of medicine was one of the fields of Byzantine life that owed a considerable amount to the Arabs, and it had no equivalent in the West throughout the Middle Ages.

So the citizens of Constantinople at all levels lived their lives very much within a framework of state control, and with an ever-present religious background. Yet, it must have been a city of strong contrasts. The whole state was seen as being under the protection of Christ, the Virgin and the saints, and this guardianship was considered to apply even to the humblest objects of everyday life. Loaves of bread were stamped with religious subjects, weights in the shops often had religious depictions, bales of cloth had lead seals attached to them which showed Christ or the Virgin. Yet alongside this pervasive and sincere devotion to Orthodox Christianity there ran a stream of great cruelty. Even though the concept of a punishment having to be humane was unknown anywhere in the Middle Ages, the Byzantines gained a reputation for extreme brutality. Long-term imprisonment was rare as a penalty for crime, but mutilation — cutting off the nose or ears, or slitting the tongue — was relatively common. Blinding was one means of rendering a rival harmless, and this fate befell eight emperors.

Further contrasts in the life of Constantinople could be found at every step, as there were no 'rich quarters' or 'poor quarters' in the city: hovels were built up against large town houses and palaces, and churches and monasteries were established wherever their donors found sites. In contrast to the planned Mese, much of the city must have been a jumble of all kinds of buildings of a wide range of periods and styles.

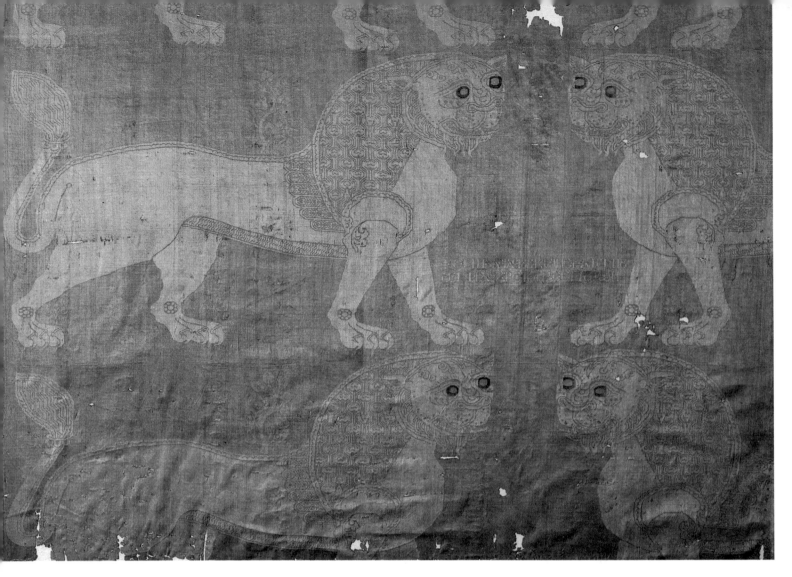

The production and sale of silk formed a very important part of the economy of Constantinople, but because of its nature, very little has survived. The silk shown here is one of a small group of woven silk fragments with a pattern of stylized lions. Their inscriptions make it possible to date them to between 976 and 1025. Their heavy weight and the scale of the design suggests that they were intended to be used as wall hangings.

Opposite left: This carved relief of a mythological centaur playing a lyre is a reminder of the important part played by music in the secular life of the citizens of Constantinople. While we know nothing of the kind of music that was played in real life, we do know that dancing girls, like the one shown here, appeared in the ceremonies of the court and hippodrome. Other instruments were flutes and a form of organ.

This sense of contrast would also have extended to the sights and sounds of the city. From the fifth century the dignified Roman toga was abandoned in favour of long coats of stiff material; for the rich and for formal occasions these were richly patterned with brocade, and probably derived ultimately from Chinese court costume. They could be very elaborate, and were later set off by strange head-dresses, swelling turbans, or peaked hats trimmed with fur. The natural contrasts between the rich and the poor, apparent in any medieval city, in Constantinople would have been further emphasized by these colourful costumes. They would have also shown up the sombre black robes of the many priests and monks moving about the city. In addition, it must always be remembered how cosmopolitan a city Constantinople was, and in all the public areas — the main streets, forums and quays of the Golden Horn — the thousands of foreigners always present in the city would have been readily identifiable by their appearance.

Perhaps the quality of any past civilization most difficult to recapture is that of its *sounds*. Anywhere that horse-drawn carts or carriages are used has a high level of noise, and when the wheels had metal rims, and were driven over roads made of stone blocks, as were those of Constantinople, the noise must have been deafening. Horses and donkeys were used a great deal, and there must have been much wheeled traffic in all the main streets for much of the day. This, combined with the cries of street sellers and shopkeepers and all the other hubbub of commercial life in a busy street or square, must have been very noisy indeed. To move from the street to the peaceful interior of one of the hundreds of churches in the city, where only faint sound would filter in from the outside world, would have offered one of the most dramatic of the many contrasts which Constantinople could provide.

Above: Another aspect of the control that the Byzantine city officials exercised over the day-to-day life of the people of the city was the selling of all commodities by the correct weight and under proper conditions.
This is a twelfth-century bread stamp of the kind that was used to mark all loaves sold publicly within the city.

Left: This relief carving may have formed part of the decoration of a palace in Constantinople. Although the peacock was a religious symbol, it can also be found in secular decoration, and the style of this relief suggests that it must date from the eleventh or twelfth century.

IMAGERY
AND ICONOCLASM

Above: Tenth-century reliquary cross and chain, with enamel image of the Virgin praying and two saints.

Left: A characteristic example of an icon, dating around 1300, with four well-known subjects painted on wood, with much use of gilding. The scenes shown are the Annunciation, the Nativity, the Baptism of of Christ and the Transfiguration, and so form part of the cycle of the Twelve Major Feasts of the Church's year.

Just as the modern mind cannot easily understand the Byzantine passion for religious controversy, so also it is hard to grasp the profound importance which the Byzantines attributed to imagery. For them, the image had a reality and an identity that perhaps can now only be found among primitive societies. Yet the Byzantine attitude to the image, far from being primitive, was immensely sophisticated, and involved a whole range of intellectual considerations including metaphysics, concern with the physical properties of light and colour, theology and symbolism.

As is the case with so much of Byzantine culture, the roots of this attitude went back to late antiquity. In the second and third century the practice of treating the emperor's image with the same respect as would be paid to his person had developed; in a conquered city the population would accept the Caesar's authority by paying homage to his image, in front of which lights and incense might be burning. In later Roman art, the most important figures were distinguished by being depicted with haloes.

Artists were highly respected members of society. By a decree of 337 they were exempted from all forms of public service, 'on condition that they devote their time to learning their crafts; by this means they may become more proficient themselves, and also train their sons'. Those exempted included architects, carpenters, silversmiths, builders, painters, sculptors, goldsmiths, glassmakers, ivory-carvers and mosaicists.

Later books of instructions indicate that artists were expected to lead exemplary lives. They were required to spend some time in prayer before they began each day's work. In this way they could concentrate all their artistic powers on the production of painted representations which would convey a genuinely spiritual message. It would be wrong to think of these artists as 'inspired' in the way that it is common to think of artists since the Renaissance. Their creative impulse was channelled into forms of art for which strong traditions had grown up, and in which artistic originality would appear only in aspects of style, or in particular brilliance of execution; the subject matter was to a large extent dictated by tradition and custom. It would be equally wrong to think of Byzantine art as fixed and unchanging, since over the centuries there were major developments in style and composition, but it was the art of an essentially conservative society, and the art of that society embodied and preserved its religious beliefs.

The fact that artists were working within a strong tradition must also account for another common characteristic of the artists of the Middle Ages: they were not for the most part interested in perpetuating their names. It is only by chance that the names of a handful of Byzantine artists who worked before the fourteenth century are known. Thereafter the numbers of artists

This small but exquisite gold reliquary of the eleventh century is a superb example of the Byzantine enameller's art. It would have been worn on a cord round the neck of the owner, bringing protection from harm; the prayer of the Virgin to Christ, which the image and its inscription conveys, would have been be seen as forming a counterpart to the prayer of the possessor.

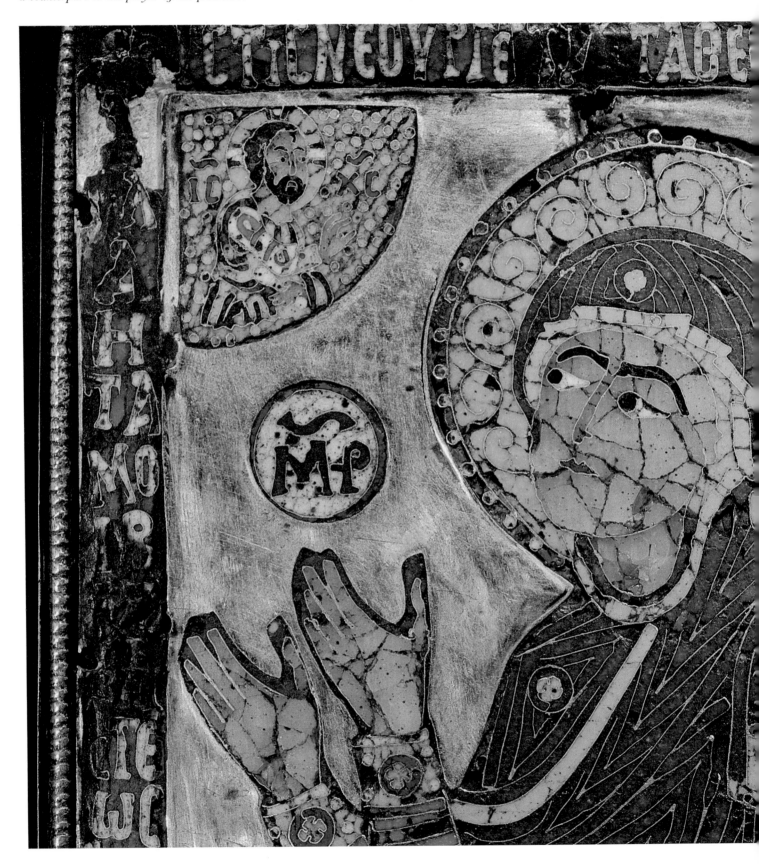

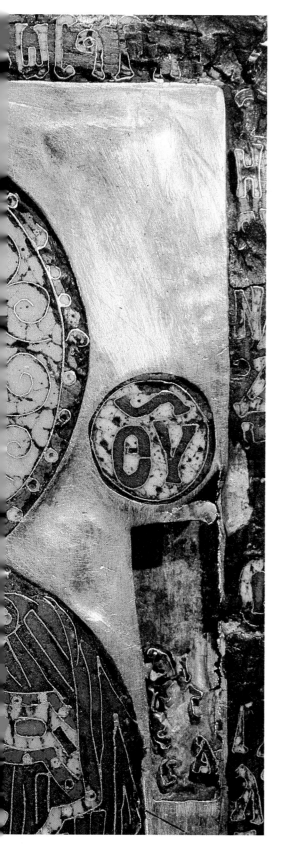

who signed their works began to increase. But the fact remains that all the great works of Byzantine art — the mosaics and frescoes, the book-covers and reliquaries in gold and enamel, the brilliantly illuminated manuscripts, the icons — were produced by individuals whose names and personalities are completely unknown to us. This readiness on the part of artists to immerse themselves in a great artistic tradition also made possible the formation of teams of craftsmen of great individual talent, working under the guidance of a leader, or master-craftsman, who between them produced the many mosaic and fresco schemes of Constantinople and the Empire. It would have been impossible for an individual to produce works on such a scale by himself, and so some form of corporate organization was essential. It can hardly be pure chance that the disintegration of the mosaic tradition largely coincided with the advent of the new Renaissance concept of artistic individuality that spread from Western Europe. While other factors were also no doubt present, the concept of a team of artists, or even of one artist working through the efforts of a team that he organized, became more and more foreign to later centuries, only surviving in relatively specialized forms.

Yet the links with ancient Rome, of which the Byzantines were so proud, created a number of problems for them. For of course Rome had been pagan, and so this new Christian society, while acknowledging its overriding debt to Rome, was at the same time concerned that its own art forms should not be too reminiscent of its pagan heritage.

It was for this reason that from its foundation, Constantinople saw relatively little new sculpture in the round. While relief sculpture was acceptable (although even then it was mainly non-figurative) statues were

almost without exception the work of earlier centuries, and of non-Christian subjects. The only new statues to be produced were of living people — emperors, important citizens, successful charioteers, and so on. For religious art, other forms had to be found.

Painting, which had always played a part in the representational arts of antiquity, began to have a more important position in religious art. This applied to painting both on portable panels and on the walls of buildings. The quest for different forms also gave rise to a much increased use of mosaic, which was to become one of the great glories of Byzantium.

From the portraiture of late antiquity was developed what is now called the icon. This is simply a form of the Greek word *eikon*, meaning 'image', and it was to embody all the new concepts relating to imagery as they evolved during the early centuries of Byzantium. There was always a certain amount of controversy about the approach that should be taken to images; there are writings from the fourth and fifth centuries which show that the early Church fathers were divided on the correct approach to the subject. There were two main objections to the use of imagery for religious purposes. Firstly, there was the well known Old Testament prohibition of 'graven images', and Constantinople was close to the Eastern Mediterranean where this attitude was endemic. Secondly, it was held by some that to depict Christ in earthly materials of wood, plaster and colours amounted to a denial of his divinity. And if this was true of Christ, then it would also apply to the saints. A true image had to be 'consubstantial' with its model in every respect, and so the only correct way to 'represent' Christ was in the consecrated bread and wine of the liturgy.

Those who defended the idea of imagery argued that an icon was a kind of symbol which reminded the onlooker of its prototype without actually reproducing it. And St Basil in the fourth century expressed the different view in defense of icons – that as the portrait had a form of identity with its prototype, so honour paid to the portrait was passed on to the prototype — as was dishonour.

These arguments rumbled on into the eighth century. For much of this time the use of icons had been getting more and more widespread, and they had begun to play a large part in church services and in private devotions. Charges of idolatry, or 'image-worship' in its crudest form, were being made. This was the position when, in 726, what has come to be called the 'iconoclast controversy' broke on Constantinople and the Empire. Its

According to the theory of the icon that the Byzantines developed, the worshipper could enter into a relationship with the spirit of the subject represented. By communicating through the medium of this fourteenth-century image, the worshipper passed on his honour to the Archangel Michael in heaven. All icons therefore had to be of frontally represented figures, and would invariably have their names beside them.

first phase lasted until 780, and there was a further period from 814 to 842. During these two phases, a systematic destruction of all figurative imagery took place. The centre of activity of the iconoclasts (as the breakers of images were called) was Constantinople, and the losses there must have been enormous. Centres further away from the capital were less affected, and it is doubtless for this reason that the finest examples of fifth and sixth century mosaics are now to be found in the exarchate of Ravenna, which was a kind of colony of Constantinople, and — even more remote — in the Monastery of St Catherine in the Sinai desert. This site, and the Church of San Vitale in Ravenna, give the best idea of what mosaic art in Constantinople in the age of Justinian was like.

One of the most powerful figures in the initiation of the first phase of iconoclasm was the Emperor Leo III, and it is interesting that he was of Syrian extraction. The influence of Islamic thought, with its traditional antipathy to figurative art, was a recurrent factor during the controversy. Another factor that may have precipitated the crisis was a siege of Constantinople by the Arabs that took place in 717; the fortunes of the whole empire were at a low ebb at that time, and it was felt that this was a sign of God's disfavour at the worship of images.

When images of Christ and the saints were hacked away from the walls and cupolas of churches, they were usually replaced either by the cross, or — for larger areas of wall — by designs of natural forms such as vine-scrolls and trees, with animals and birds. In the apse of the huge church of St Irene the cross still exists from the days of iconoclasm, and in a small, vaulted room in part of the upper structure of Hagia Sophia it can be seen that mosaic roundels, which once contained portrait busts of saints, now only show crosses, and the area of mosaic which held each saint's name is now blank.

As in other religious matters, sides were taken with passionate intensity of feeling, and lines of theological battle were drawn. Throughout the iconoclast period it was the monasteries that were chief defenders of images.

Indeed, a secondary reason for the conflict was that young men could avoid military service by becoming monks, and the Emperor could see the many monasteries of Constantinople filled with able-bodied men who thus became exempt from call-up to the Army. Within the forces, it was the Navy, whose personnel came largely from the Aegean coasts, who favoured the use of icons, while the Army, mainly composed of Asiatics and Syrians, supported the iconoclasts. Women were prominent among the *iconodules*, as the defenders of icons were called. When Leo III ordered the removal and destruction of the great icon of Christ over the Chalke Gate of the Great Palace, a crowd of enraged women, having heard what was happening, rushed to the scene and upset the ladder of the soldiers who were removing it, killing the man who had climbed up it. According to some accounts they were led by a patrician lady called Mary, while others say that their leader was a nun called Theodosia, who was later martyred in the hippodrome. It was while there were powerful empresses on the throne that iconoclasm was stopped — under the Empress Irene the Athenian in 780 and under the Empress Theodora, the widow of Theophilus, in 842.

The historian Theophanes tells a story about the Empress Theodora, the wife of the Emperor Theophilus. One day the court fool, called Denderis, came unexpectedly into the Empress's apartments in the imperial palace (these would usually have been completely barred to men, with only women and eunuchs being allowed there, but the position of Denderis, who may have been a dwarf, was clearly different). There he found the Empress kissing an icon. When he asked her what it was she had in her hands, she replied that it was one of her beautiful dolls, and she was kissing it because she loved it so much. A little later Theophilus asked Denderis what news he had of activities in the palace, and Denderis told the Emperor what he had seen in Theodora's apartments. The Emperor realized what had happened, and went at once to the Empress's rooms. In a rage, he burst in and accused her of practising idolatry. Theodora, with great self-possession, said that the fool had only seen her and her maids looking in their mirrors, and their faces reflected there. Although he was not completely convinced, the Emperor withdrew. It was generally women who took risks in maintaining their use of icons, and it would seem that the iconoclasts' charges of idolatry were not always without foundation.

The day on which it was finally decreed that it was once again permissible to own, display and use icons in worship was one of great rejoicing in Constantinople. The event is still commemorated all over the Orthodox world on the first Sunday in Lent, which is known as the 'Feast of Orthodoxy'; there are even icons of the celebration of this feast.

The iconoclast controversy can be seen as a kind of microcosm of the Byzantine cultural outlook. The arguments put forward by each side, and the intensity with which these differing views were held, the way that all levels of society were affected by a relatively abstruse theological argument, the ramifications of the dispute into political life, the implicit importance that was accorded to imagery by the very nature of the controversy — all of these reveal aspects of the Byzantine personality.

Even before the dispute reached its height in the eighth century, the style in which Byzantine artists created religious works had changed significantly from the style of the fourth and fifth centuries, which was still often reminiscent of late antiquity. Artists were clearly trying to work towards a stylistic formula in which both the human figure and whole compositions could be represented in a way that would fulfil two opposing criteria. A painting had to be recognizable as a representation of its subject, but it must avoid the naturalism inherent in pagan art. It was one of the positive results of the iconoclast dispute that out of all the highly repetitive arguments used by both sides there emerged a coherent 'theory of the icon'.

This beautifully coloured floor mosaic is a reminder of the untold wealth of secular art that could have been found at any one time in Constantinople. This particular detail is from the Great Palace of the emperors, and probably dates from the sixth century. It provides yet another illustration of the perpetual admiration in which the Byzantine held so many of the themes of classical art.

According to this theory, which applied only to religious imagery, every representation or portrait was a kind of emanation of its prototype; it was identical as regards its *essence*, but was different as regards its *substance*. Because it had a form of identity with its subject, it was regarded as a sort of receptacle, or vessel, for the spirit of the original. But for this to be the case the image had to be created in the correct way — that is, it had to contain the known characteristics of the original, and, so that there could be no doubt, the name or subject had to be written beside it. If these requirements were met, the image or icon became itself worthy of veneration to the same extent as its prototype.

The effect that this thinking had on all Byzantine art was profound. The interior of every church in Constantinople was, after the restoration of images, gradually transformed in keeping with this outlook, and private houses could once again display icons. As the years passed almost all the decoration of the iconoclast period was replaced by frescoes, mosaics and icons created in conformity with this theory.

The natural tendency of the Byzantines to think in strongly hieratic terms was inevitably applied to their religious art, and so they developed a complex arrangement of the mosaics and frescoes in their churches that made each church into a microcosm of the Christian universe. The interior of the cupola would usually have held a representation of Christ, as the most important image in the church. The Virgin occupied the apse; this was the next most significant area of the building, and so was given the next image in the 'hierarchy of sanctity'. In the third 'zone' — usually the areas of the building that supported the dome — came representations of the main feasts of the Christian year. Finally, in the lower parts of the church — round the walls, in niches, on the inside faces of arches — were numerous depictions of individual saints. The interiors of the church buildings in Constantinople which still stand, such as the Budrum Djami and the Gül Djami, would all originally have displayed this system of imagery.

No complete interior has survived, though that of the Kariye Djami, from the early fourteenth century, shows least damage. But if any large number of church interiors from the tenth to twelfth centuries had survived, it is likely that no two would be found to be alike. While all would have conformed in some measure to the same general pattern, there would have been individual variations due to the dedication of the church, the wishes of the donor, the chance irregularities of the building due to earlier restorations, and so on.

The theory of the icon also explains why all Byzantine religious imagery is completely frontal and still. The beholder had to enter into a relationship with the icon in order to honour the original subject. This could only be achieved if the image 'looked at him' and received the spiritual message that his prayer contained. An icon in which the portrait had its eyes closed, or in which a figure showed only a back or profile view, would have been useless, as the subject was effectively 'not present'. The only figures ever shown in profile in Byzantine religious art are those not considered worthy of veneration, like Judas Iscariot or the Pharisees.

An appropriate artistic style was also developed for religious art. The human figure was shown as a dematerialized, rather abstracted form, with clothing often fashioned into arbitrary, jagged patterns. The spiritual aspect of the figure could be suggested by no indication of a ground level (conveying a sense of the weightlessness of the subject), by attenuated proportions, and by exaggeratedly large eyes.

But it is important to realize that this style was reserved for religious imagery. It would have been found in any church or monastery in Constantinople, in the figures in fresco and mosaic on the walls and in the cupolas, and in the icons displayed on the screens, all staring down at the clergy

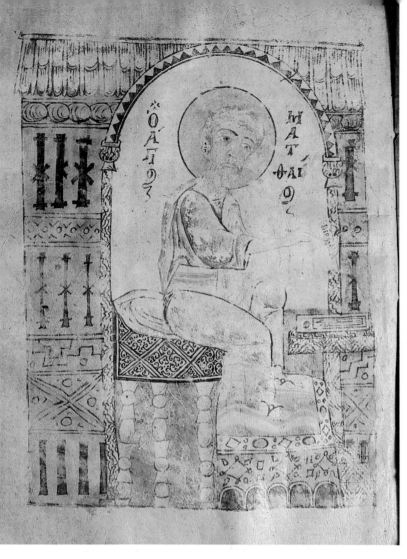

and the participants as they enacted the sacred drama of the liturgy.

For secular art, the situation was very different. It is clear that there were no such inhibitions as have just been described when it came to the decoration of a palace, or the embellishment of silver plates and drinking vessels for the use of wealthy patricians or merchants. By great good fortune part of a mosaic floor from the Great Palace of Constantinople has been discovered. It probably dates from the later sixth century, and shows a range of completely secular subjects. Almost all have a strongly classical character, and they are depicted with a robust verve that speaks a completely different artistic language from that of the other-worldly realm of religious imagery. There are hunting scenes, pastoral episodes, and children playing, all shown against a neutral background of cream-coloured mosaic. One could be looking down on the floor of a Roman palace of late antiquity; indeed, the fact that these mosaics are on a floor is itself an indication of a surviving Hellenistic stream of artistic style that ran parallel with the more 'spiritual' art used for religious purposes. Figural mosaics in church buildings were confined to upper walls, vaults and cupolas from the early centuries of Christian art, with floors normally displaying only abstract designs. This is the only such floor that has so far been discovered in the city, but there is no reason to suppose that there would not have been many others, maintaining the links with the Roman world of which the Byzantines were so proud.

While the exact date of the Great Palace floor mosaic is still not completely certain, there is another class of secular art about which there is no doubt. This is decorated silver. It was mentioned earlier that the Byzantines stamped many of their silver wares with punches that showed that the silver was of the correct purity, and that one of these stamps was a portrait of the reigning emperor. A whole range of silver objects has survived, much of it with official stamps dating from the early seventh century, which show that in this field too the classical tradition was still very much alive. Plates, cups, bowls and ewers with beautifully decorated surfaces, displaying lively scenes from classical mythology, episodes from Homer, and pastoral scenes, still exist — all worked in a confident, robust style, matching the mood of the subjects.

If these are compared with decorated silver made for religious use, such

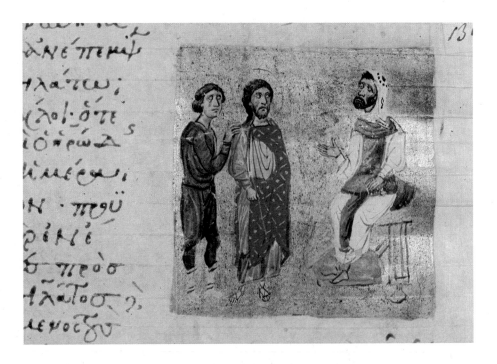

as the large patens found at Riha and Stuma, which were used for the distribution of the bread at the liturgy, it is clear that they are products of a completely different artistic world. On the patens, the staring eyes and abstracted draperies of the apostles, shown receiving the communion from Christ, illustrate perfectly a stage in the development of what is now called 'Byzantine style'. They were stamped in the later sixth century, during the reign of the Emperor Justin II. Comparisons such as this show how completely mistaken is the view of Byzantine art as being an unchanging and purely religious style. Throughout history, it is always religious art and architecture that has survived most readily. The loss of secular art in Constantinople must have been prodigious, but there is still sufficient evidence that in their palaces and houses people enjoyed the use of many beautiful artefacts, decorated with secular themes and motifs. Not only mosaic floors and silver vessels, but carved ivory boxes, textiles of all kinds and articles of personal adornment would certainly have been found in large quantities in the houses of wealthy citizens throughout most of the thousand years of the city's life.

THE
MONASTIC IDEAL

Above : Initial T from an eleventh or twelfth-century illuminated manuscript, Athens, cod. 190, fol. 31. v.

Left : Though damaged, this beautiful early fourteenth-century head of 'Melane the Nun' is one of the most striking of late Byzantine portraits. It was incorporated into a large devotional mosaic in the Kariye Djami under the patronage of Theodore Metochites, but the precise identity of the subject is not certain. Many members of the ruling and aristocratic classes of Constantinople chose to enter monasteries or convents, and so leave behind them the cares and problems of authority, possessions or noble birth.

Overleaf, above : Miniature of St Paul holding a scroll. From an eleventh-century manuscript illuminated in a monastery, as were most such manuscripts. Athens, cod. 149, fol. 103. r.

Overleaf below : This early fourteenth-century mosaic in the Parecclesion of the Kariye Djami is from the tomb of Michael Tornikes and his wife, who became the nun Eugenia in her old age.

To establish a true picture of life in Constantinople it is important to realize how greatly monks — and indeed all those whose lives were clearly dominated by religious ideals — were respected. The hundreds of monasteries which are known to have existed in the city held at any one time scores of thousands of monks. While this was symptomatic of the importance of religion throughout Europe during the medieval period, monasteries were much more in evidence for a much longer period in Constantinople than in Western Europe, where the numerical expansion of the monasteries was considerably later.

The popularity of monks and monastic life showed itself in a number of ways. All the Church leaders of higher rank were drawn from the monasteries, and it was possible for these men to attract a huge popular following; a modern survival of this tradition was Archbishop Makarios, who was made President of Cyprus. The advice of senior clergy was usually valued, and an emperor would only ignore it at his peril. In this respect the Byzantine tradition is closely related to those of other Middle Eastern areas: in Palestine the prophets of the Old Testament could use the weight of their moral authority to oppose the king. But besides being valued for both theological and political wisdom, the company of monks was often sought by rich and cultured members of Byzantine society for the intellectual pleasures of conversation and discussion that it provided. Monastic life offered one of the principal career openings for any well-educated man, and even if he was not ambitious in any wordly sense, the way of life could, within particular limitations, have been an agreeable one. The intellectual resources of the major monasteries of Constantinople — in terms of their libraries — would have been superior to any other of the city's institutions except, perhaps, the library of the Patriarchate. Given the generally religious tenor of all aspects of life, to enter a monastery was to take up one of a very limited set of options, and one which would guarantee security and companionship until old age and death. The same could be said of the convents of the city, although these were not so numerous.

The popularity of the monastic life was doubtless partly due to the security it provided, but probably even more to the Byzantine view of existence in this world. A person's earthly life was regarded by the Byzantines as important only to the extent that it provided the chance to prepare for life beyond the grave; to pass one's years as a monk or nun, or even as a hermit, would provide a framework for existence likely to ensure the passage of the soul to heaven after death. Indeed, a Greek phrase for embracing the religious life in any form is 'leaving the world', as if the final transition from life to death were already made. The Orthodox

Church has a special order of service for the burial of priests and monks, which is much longer and more discursive than that for laymen; frequently during the service reference is made to the imminence of death, and to how the priests who are now officiating at the burial of one of their number shall at any time have to follow him:

> We are all constrained to come to that same abode, and shall hide ourselves beneath a gravestone like to this, and shall ourselves shortly turn to dust; let us pray to Christ to give him rest who has been taken thence. For such is our life here, brethren, a mockery upon the earth . . .
> We are a fleeting dream, a breath which endures for no time, the flight of a passing bird, a ship which leaves no trace of its path upon the sea . . .

It was quite common for an influential politician, or even an emperor or other member of the imperial family, to become a monk; this might take the form of retirement in old age, or else a discreet withdrawal from public life to avoid the retribution of rivals. The monasteries and convents of Constantinople at one time or another housed many distinguished people, some going there willingly, some under duress. In 944, Romanus I Lecapenus was banished by his sons to a monastery on an island in the Sea of Marmara, and in 1081 Nicephorus III retired voluntarily to the monastery of the Peribleptos in Constantinople; Helena, the last Byzantine empress, and wife of Manuel II Palaeologus, ended her days in a convent where she had gladly gone as the nun, Hypomene.

It can be seen from this that the monasteries of Constantinople were not necessarily places of ascetic retreat. From the early centuries there had always been a distinction between the holy man, who lived as a hermit in the desert or some other remote area, and the monk who was a member of a community. Monasteries and convents could also be in unpopulated open country, but those in Constantinople would obviously have attracted monks and nuns who wished to live in more urban surroundings. A number of the most famous monastic figures in the history of the city are known to have come there from the provinces; those who wanted to maintain the more peaceful existence provided by a monastery in a small town, or in the isolation of Mount Athos, could always have done so. It is therefore quite probable that the monks in the monasteries of the city — and certainly those in the greatest of them, such as the Studios Monastery, the Pantocrator and the Peribleptos, would have been of a character to appreciate the opportunities for learning, for intellectual pursuits and for educated and civilized discussion, either with their fellow monks, or with lay friends living in the city.

It should be understood that the Orthodox Church never built up a system of monastic 'orders' such as existed in the West; all monks kept the 'rule of St Basil', which deliberately avoided the extremes of asceticism to which the hermetic tradition aspired. Hours of worship and of work were laid down, and the ideals of poverty and chastity were imposed, as in the West; the education of children, where appropriate, was also part of this rule. Orthodox monks still live today by the rule of St Basil.

So it can be seen that the monasteries of Constantinople, numbering altogether in hundreds, would have answered the needs of a considerable proportion of the educated population of the city. Combining as it did the qualities of a tradition of learning with aspirations to a spiritual life, the monastic ideal represented a fulfilment of the needs of life for many Byzantines.

But monasteries and convents took the form that they did in the Byzantine world because there was another outlet for those seeking a more remote and extreme form of religious life; this was the life of the hermit or anchorite. While not usually men of great learning, the spiritual wisdom of these 'solitaries', as they were called, in some cases gave them a moral authority

Pages 101 and 102 show the outer container of a tenth-century reliquary of the true cross, called a staurothèque. It is one of the richest and most elaborate ensembles of Byzantine enamels to have survived. An inscription indicates that it was made for the Proedros Basil. In 985 he was exiled and his belongings were confiscated. This cross was taken away from Constantinople in 1207 by one of the German leaders of the Western forces that sacked the city in 1204, and it has been in Germany ever since. It is made of gold and cloisonné enamel throughout, with many precious stones. The detail (left) of the enthroned Christ shows the extraordinary skill of the Byzantine craftsmen; gold strips were formed into the required shapes and soldered into the sunken area of gold. These 'enclosures' were then filled with the enamel in powdered form, and heated in a kiln until the enamel (a form of coloured glass) melted and fused. The other details show the complex programme of imagery that was appropriate to such a sacred relic. Christ is surrounded by the apostles and other saints, mainly bishops.

that brought them the respect and devotion of thousands. Known as 'holy men' (the Greek word is *hosios* as distinct from the word for saint, *hagios*), they have a particular and greatly admired place in the Orthodox world. (Indeed, the earliest monks were also hermits, seeking solitary life in the Egyptian desert in the fourth century, who later formed small communities leading a more communal kind of life under the aegis of St Anthony.)

Hermits took the decision to 'leave the world' and install themselves in a remote and inaccessible area because they believed that only through extreme self-denial — the abnegation not only of worldly goods, but even of human contact and companionship and of the relative security that went with it — could they achieve a form of realization which would bring its own spiritual reward. Even today, the cliffs on the tip of the promontory of Mount Athos are the home of a number of hermits living in tiny huts perched on ledges of rock. These are the survivors of a tradition of ascetic life that reaches back to the earliest centuries of Byzantium. The spiritual fulfilment they sought was not of the kind that could be achieved in any

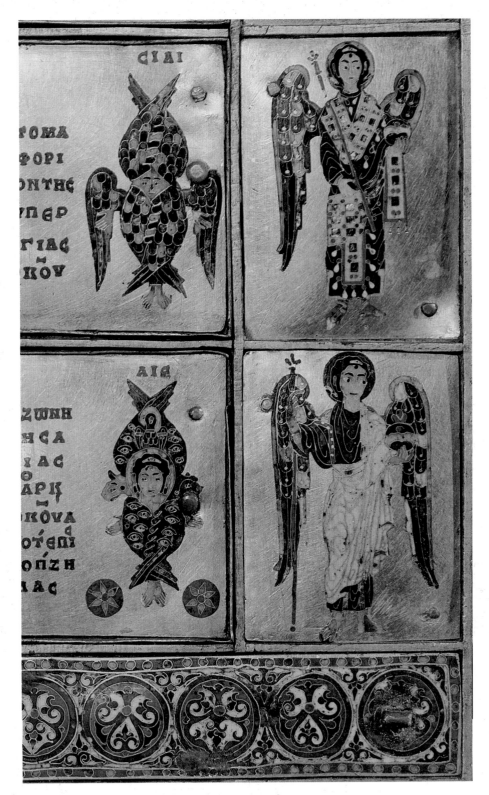

community, with a corporate life of prayer and the sharing of communal tasks, but could come only from solitary contemplation and a complete withdrawal from worldly concerns. From the fourth and fifth centuries there is a written work known as *The Sayings of the Fathers*, in which the particular wisdom of these earliest hermits is perpetuated. One of the sayings illustrates the purpose for which many of these solitaries embarked on their way of life. St Anthony was asked by a philosopher how, being a man of such learning and insight, he could survive without the comfort provided by books. The holy man answered: 'My book, philosopher, is the nature of all created things; as often as I wish to read the words of God, they are here beside me'.

Above: Monastery of Dochiariou, Mount Athos, seen from the sea.

Right and far right: The extreme unworldliness and asceticism of the stylites made them the object of veneration throughout the Empire. These two images show the artistic convention that grew up for depicting them. Both are of the earliest and most famous of all 'column dwellers', St Simeon Stylites. The relief is from the fifth or sixth century, and shows the saint being visited by a man climbing a ladder and holding what is probably a censer. The mosaic is in St Marks, Venice, and dates from the thirteenth century. There are also illustrations of stylites letting down a basket on a length of rope; this would presumably have been for their small supplies of food, and for other needs — some certainly maintained quite an active correspondence.

For the most part these 'solitaries' would not have been in evidence at all in Constantinople, as their existence was tied to the empty and desert places of the Mediterranean. In their most extreme form, however, they did exist in the city, at least from time to time; these were hermits whose desire to leave the cares of the world behind, and at the same time to be as close as possible to God, drove them to spending their lives on the tops of columns. They were called 'stylites', or column-dwellers. The earliest of these, St Simeon Stylites, lived in the fourth century near Antioch; his fame became enormous, and thousands of pilgrims came to hear him speaking from the top of his column.

There must at different times have been many hundreds of these stylites. In the fifth century, just outside Constantinople, St Daniel Stylites lived on a column from the age of forty-seven until his death at the age of eighty-four. He was a very well-known personality in the city, and very much revered, being credited with remarkable powers of healing. The Emperor Theodosius II became concerned at the stylite's continued exposure, and whenever there had been a storm would send to ask how he was. One winter night, a particularly violent gale blew away the stylite's only cover — a piece of animal skin. When next morning he made no response to calls from the ground, ladders were set up, and he was found to be alive, but frozen so stiff that he was unable to stand or speak. After this episode he allowed the Emperor to have a small shelter erected on the top of his column to provide slight protection from rain and snow. On one occasion he was persuaded to come down from his column to deliver a personal rebuke to a member of the imperial family for expressing heretical views. Huge crowds followed him, and he had to be sheltered from them.

Also in the fifth century, a stylite called John apparently lived on a column in the heart of the complex of government buildings, at the Hebdomon. There is also a record of a tenth-century stylite who suffered from the insecurity of his way of life when, during a severe earthquake, his column near to the Sea of Marmara, in the Eutropius district of the city, collapsed and threw him into the waves. Even in 1204 stylites still existed, as there is from that date the marvelling description by a Western knight, Robert of Clari, who wrote in his account of the Fourth Crusade that on the two huge columns erected in the early centuries of the city's life by the Emperors Theodosius and Arcadius which had originally carried statues, there were now instead two stylites: 'On each of these columns', he wrote, 'lived a hermit in a little hut that was on them, and you could see a door at the base of these columns, by which you could climb them.'

It is true that columns of exceptional size such as these would have been built with spiral staircases inside them, but there is plenty of evidence, both in the recorded lives of stylites and in visual records such as paintings and carved reliefs, that it was more usual for ladders to be used by anyone who wished to approach them. This was of course necessary when the stylite died and had to be taken down for burial. Conversation would have been difficult to carry on with someone on the top of a column thirty or forty feet high, and often confession, or advice of an intimate nature was sought; for instance, the tenth century empress Helena Lacapena was advised by the stylite known as St Basil the Less how to have a son.

So when trying to visualize the appearance of Constantinople, and the life that went on there, it is important to keep in mind the extensive part played by monastic life. While stylites would have been seen infrequently, they nevertheless represented a supreme example of asceticism and spirituality which was very much a Byzantine ideal. This aspect of life in the city must have contrasted sharply with the worldly bargaining and commercial trafficking that went on ceaselessly in the shops and bazaars, and on the quays of the Golden Horn.

Today the major survival of Byzantine monasticism is the autonomous group of monasteries on Mount Athos. This is the name of one of the peninsulas of Chalkidike where some twenty-four monasteries are still in existence. There it is possible to glimpse something of the quality of life that attracted such large numbers of Byzantines to 'leave the world'. Here, the monastery of Xeropotamou is seen from the land.

EPILOGUE: THE OTTOMAN CONQUEST AND AFTER

For the Byzantines, the fifteenth century was a period of growing desperation. Weakened by damaging internal strife throughout the previous century, they watched the rolling flood of Turkish power slowly engulf what was left of their Empire. Time and again they tried to rally political and military support from the Western powers to defend them from the infidel. In 1400 the Emperor Manuel II Palaeologus even visited England to ask for help from King Henry IV, and passed Christmas day with the royal household in the palace at Eltham. There, as well as in Italy and France, where he had also been received, he made a great personal impression by his dignity and learning, but it was all to no avail. He returned to Constantinople empty-handed.

For a long time the Byzantine emperors had realized that help from the West would be much more readily forthcoming if religious union between the Greek and Roman Churches could be achieved. Several Church councils had attempted this; the last and most famous, at which both the Emperor John VIII Palaeologus and the Greek Patriarch, Joseph, were present, was held in Ferrara and Florence in 1438—39. By then the question of union had become a major international issue, as the Turkish threat loomed over all of Europe. Agreement on all the points of theological difference was finally pushed through, and the Greeks returned to Constantinople.

But it was one thing to sign an agreement on union, which inevitably had involved major theological concessions to the Roman Church, and quite another to have it accepted and implemented in the churches of Constantinople. Most of the Greek bishops refused to be bound by the signatures of their delegates, and the citizens showed a typical Greek obstinacy in refusing to give up any of their creed or the liturgical customs that had sustained them for over a thousand years. All that the Emperor had achieved was, for them, a source of bitterness and division. There could be no better example of the readiness of the Byzantines to buy peace in the hereafter at the expense of physical hardship and danger in this world. In religious matters the currency of expediency had no value for them.

The grip of the Turks on the city was slowly tightening. With hindsight it is clear that for some decades the city had been doomed to fall to them — the only uncertainty was when the moment of destruction would arrive. At the time, it was innate Byzantine fatalism which was most apparent — the

Islamic minarets and domes are now the most prominent features of the skyline of the city founded by Constantine, but the harbour of the Golden Horn in the foreground of this view is still in use after over two thousand years.

Above: Initial E from a late eleventh or early twelfth-century manuscript, Athens, cod. 190, fol. 22. v.

fatalism which held that the loss of Constantinople (if such a tragedy should occur) would be a just punishment for the sins of its people. The circumstances only needed the combination of a few factors to precipitate the end. In the ambitious and talented young Sultan, Mehmet II, the Turks had a leader with all the necessary qualities, and their empire could provide the resources required for such a huge military undertaking. If there was one moment in which the fate of Constantinople was finally sealed it could be said to have been when, in the summer of 1452, a brilliant Hungarian engineer called Urban offered his services as a cannon-founder to the last Byzantine Emperor, Constantine XI Dragases. The Emperor could not afford to pay Urban the fee he demanded, so Urban immediately offered his services to the Sultan. After producing a trial cannon, Urban, at a salary four times as great as he had asked, was commissioned by Mehmet to cast the biggest cannon the world had yet seen, almost 9 metres (29 ft) long, which fired cannon-balls weighing 635 kilos (1400 lbs). No walls could withstand bombardment by this monstrous weapon for very long.

So, with the fatal inevitability of a classical Greek drama, the end of the city drew near. During April of 1453, the Turkish army under the personal command of the Sultan was installing itself under the walls of Constantinople, and the siege began. By the end of May the end was in sight. On Monday the 28th, it became clear to the defenders that the final assault must now be imminent.

Above left, and right: It was superb and costly pieces such as these which formed much of the booty that the Venetians brought back from Constantinople after the Fourth Crusade of 1204. The onyx chalice with silver-gilt mounts, enamels and pearls, probably dates from the tenth century. The relief icon of St Michael is a unique work and must always have been highly prized. It probably dates from the eleventh century. Both are now in the Treasury of St Mark's, Venice. It is one of the ironies of history that had these and many other such works not been looted they might not have survived the final sack of the city in 1453, and so might have vanished altogether. They are a powerful and evocative reminder of the glories achieved by the Byzantines during the centuries of their greatness.

The Turkish encampments were silent on that day, as the soldiers rested before the last battle, but inside the city there was still activity. Not only were armaments and supplies being distributed, but processions were formed as icons and relics were brought out and carried by the faithful to the parts of the walls where the Turkish cannons had caused most damage. All the Byzantines — men, women and children — were united in these final efforts — the desperation of a doomed people comes through all the eye-witness accounts of the fall of the city. There were many Italians among the beseiged; as most of them did not have their families with them, they could devote themselves to the defence without other distractions, and they played a heroic part in the final act of the drama.

Unity came too in another form that evening. For five months — ever since the Latin rite had been forced on them as the price of Western aid — no Greek had entered Hagia Sophia. Now, in these last dark hours of Christian rule in the city of Constantine, all differences were forgotten. Everyone who was not involved in the actual defence of the walls crowded into Hagia Sophia — Greek priests and bishops, some of whom had accepted union and others who had refused to compromise, Catalans, Greeks, Italians, even the Cardinal, Isidore, who had presided over the hated union,

*Left: The Gül Djami (or 'Rose Mosque')
is one of the many churches of Constantinople
to be turned into mosques by the Turks
after 1453. According to a strong tradition,
it was this church that was the first to be
entered by the victorious Turks, and was
therefore the church dedicated to St Theodosia.
The view of the apse seen here will have
remained virtually unchanged since that day.*

*Right: A fascination with the effects of light
was one of the most enduring interests of
the Byzantines. Although this evocative
image of shadows cast on a marble column is
from St Mark's in Venice, it could have
been matched in many of the churches of
Constantinople throughout the centuries of
Christian rule.*

all came to the altar to receive the sacrament side by side, as the last Christian ceremony that was to be enacted under Justinian's dome took place.

The Emperor had called his ministers and commanders together that evening, and after a short speech he took his leave of them, asking each for their forgiveness if, in the tensions of the last months, he had given offence. Then he too joined in the worship in the Great Church. After returning to the palace at Blachernae he bid farewell to his household, and spent the last remaining hours of the night riding along the length of the great land walls that had served the city so well for over 1000 years, seeing that all that could be done was done in readiness for their defence. Then, between one and two in the morning, the Turks launched their final assault.

The outcome could not have been long in doubt; within about five hours the city was taken. The pillage and slaughter were appalling. According to Muslim custom, if a city did not submit before a siege was begun, its eventual conquerors were allowed three days to plunder it; the victorious Turkish forces began immediately to do this. Houses, shops, churches, monasteries and convents — within a matter of hours all had been entered and looted.

Left: Eleventh-century illustration of the exodus from a burning city. Cynegetica of Pseudo-Oppian; cod. gr. 479, fol. 42. r.

Right: Eleventh-century mosaic of weeping women from the scene of the Deposition, in the Baptistry of St Mark's.
These images of sorrow and loss convey something of the human impact of the catastrophe of the capture of Constantinople by the Turks. While it is more often the historical significance of the final conquest of the city of Constantine that is emphasized, it should not be forgotten that for the inhabitants and the many foreign defenders who survived, the personal disasters would have been overwhelming.

Yet still the Byzantines believed that a last miracle might save them. In Hagia Sophia the services of the night were over, but the vast church was still crowded with worshippers who had continued their devotions with the morning service of matins. They barred the great bronze doors when the Turkish troops poured into the courtyard, but it was no use. The doors were broken down and Muslim soldiers rushed into the holiest and most famous church in Eastern Christendom. The priests were still chanting the service at the altar as the Turks first killed the oldest and most infirm of the worshippers, then bound the women into groups with their own scarves and led them back to the Turkish encampment. Next, they plundered the gold and silver vessels and ornaments. Truly the reign of anti-Christ, about which there was an old Byzantine legend, had now come to pass.

An eye-witness left a record of the events in another church — that of St Theodosia, now called the Gül Djami, or 'Rose Mosque'. The feast day of the saint particularly revered by women is celebrated on the 29th of May, and in spite of the imminent Turkish attack the women of the quarter had decorated their church profusely with roses, then in their short but abundant season. In the dawn hours the first band of Turkish sailors to enter the city burst into the church to find it crowded with Greek women and children taking refuge there and beginning the first service of the day.

There, under the newly-cut roses, the women were shared out among the victors and led away. This account is perpetuated in the name given to the building when it was turned into a mosque.

Throughout the first part of the day fighting continued in isolated areas, but soon all resistance had been overcome. The Emperor himself — Constantine XI — died in a breach of the wall made by the huge cannon, fighting heroically to stem the flood of Turkish soldiers pouring through. His body was never identified for certain, although it was said that his mutilated corpse had been found among a pile of the slain, distinguished by the eagle that was embroidered on his purple boots. He certainly has no known grave. His death in these circumstances confirmed an ancient Byzantine superstition, that the city would finally fall when an emperor with the same name as its founder was on the throne.

It was not until evening that the Sultan finally entered the city. He rode right through its length from the land walls to Hagia Sophia. Not yet twenty-four years old, he had captured the stronghold of Christendom that had defied the world for over a thousand years. Outside Hagia Sophia he knelt down, picked up a handful of earth, and sprinkled it over his turban as an act of humility before the God who had allowed him this stupendous victory. Then he went into the Great Church, where he at once had the Muslim faith proclaimed from the pulpit; from then on, the building was a mosque. Later that evening he went across to the ruins of the old palace of the emperors; as he wandered among the crumbling buildings, through which the currents of history had flowed for so many centuries, he was heard to say to himself two lines of Persian verse which can serve as an epitaph on the grave of the brilliant civilization of the Byzantines:

> The spider weaves the curtains in the palace of the Caesars;
> The owl calls the watches in Afrasiab's towers.

While the everyday life of the city would have changed at once, with Turkish turbans being seen everywhere, and the old patterns of trade and commerce completely disrupted, architecturally, the city only very gradually took on the character of an Islamic centre. The Sultan respected the Greeks for their learning and for their religion, and he wanted them to remain as a self-governing Christian community within his empire. To this end he gave the citizens a new constitution, by which their leader would be the patriarch, who would be responsible to him for their good behaviour.

Mehmet II's original intention was that the inhabitants should retain all their churches for their own use with the exception of Hagia Sophia; this he had always resolved should be annexed for Islam. The Patriarch began by living in quarters adjoining the next most holy of the churches of the city, that of the Holy Apostles, which was also the chief mausoleum of the Byzantine emperors. Amazingly, this had not been looted by the Turks. The new Patriarch, under his monastic name of Gennadius, was appointed in June 1453, and enthroned by the Sultan in January 1454. He built up a valuable relationship with Mehmet, who seems to have behaved with great tolerance and shown outstanding political wisdom in his attitude to his new subjects.

But not even the Sultan could always control the zeal of his supporters — much less his successors. One by one, churches were taken from the Greeks and given other functions, most of them being turned into mosques. The huge church of St Irene was made into an armoury, and that of St John Dippion was (with a number of others, as reported in 1499 by a Western traveller, Arnold von Harff) used as a kind of menagerie or zoo. By about 1500 many more churches and monasteries, including the Panachrantos, St Saviour in Chora and the great monastery of St. John Studion, had become mosques. Occasionally the Greeks could hold out against their

The fastidious delicacy of this fifteenth-century portrait of the Sultan Mehmet II conceals the ruthless determination which must have formed a major part of his character. Could it be that, in later life, the scent of the rose he holds reminds him of the day his troops captured and sacked the city, 29 May, 1453, when the roses were in flower?

rulers, as when, in about 1520, the Sultan Selim I, who had a strong dislike of Christians, issued an order that all their churches should be confiscated. The Patriarch employed a clever lawyer, called Xenakis, who brought before the Sultan three Turkish soldiers, each of them nearly a hundred years old. These ancient warriors swore on the Koran that they had been part of Mehmet II's bodyguard when he took the city in 1453, and had seen officials from various quarters of the city come to him and present the keys of their districts to him as a sign of surrender. Mehmet had therefore permitted them to retain their churches. Selim I felt bound by this evidence to allow the Christians to keep their remaining religious buildings.

But gradually, as minarets were built from which the *muezzin* could call the faithful to prayer, the skyline of the city began to assume its unmistakably Islamic character. This, more than any other single factor, is what gives modern Istanbul its very specific quality, causing it to share in a real sense in the cultures of both Europe and Asia. There must now be many hundreds of minarets, which collectively impose a Muslim silhouette on almost any view of the old city. Of the four minarets which now rise round Hagia Sophia, for example, one was built by Mehmet II in the years immediately after his capture of the city, one by Beyazit II late in the fifteenth century, and the other two by Selim II in the later sixteenth century. As each church became a mosque, or as each new mosque was built, so another minaret was added to those already standing. The largest mosques had four minarets, and, in the exceptional case of the famous 'Blue Mosque', six.

As the years passed the greatness of Byzantium was reflected more and more faintly in its surviving relics. The chaplain to the English Embassy, Edward Browne, wrote in 1677: 'It doth go hugely against the grain to see the crescent exalted everywhere, where the Cross stood so long triumphant.' By the eighteenth century there were only three churches left in Greek hands that had been built before the Turkish conquest. The leadership of the Orthodox Church passed to Russia, and, as in the fourth century the city founded by Constantine had been called New Rome, so Moscow was for a time referred to as the Third Rome.

It is sometimes suggested that some elements of the palace rites and ceremonies of the Byzantine emperors survived in the semi-Oriental splendour of the court of the Ottoman sultans. It is true that Mehmet II saw himself as, to some extent, the heir to the Byzantine emperors, and he did indeed build a new palace for himself. It was in a more central part of the city than any of the earlier imperial palaces, occupying land adjacent to the former forum of Theodosius. It was completed in 1457, but he seems to have lived in it for only about ten years; it had become clear that it was not large enough for use both as a private residence and as the administrative centre of a large and ever-expanding empire. So a new palace was begun on the high ground near the eastern tip of the city, and it was this site that served the sultans into modern times, being known as the Topkapi Serai.

But even if the sultans had wished to perpetuate the ceremonial of the Byzantine emperors, and if sufficient knowledge thereof had survived the declining years of the court and the sack of the city, could it have been sustained over the first decades of Turkish rule? Whatever the Ottoman intentions may have been, it seems hardly possible that there could have been anything but the most fragmentary knowledge of Byzantine court ceremonial left by the later fifteenth century, when the large new palace was coming into use.

So what survived of Byzantium?

The physical remains today are confined to the walls and a few buildings, of which Hagia Sophia is the undisputed giant. The Greek Patriarch, the

The tranquillity of this remote view of Mount Athos is as apparent today as it was when St Athanasius founded the first monastery there in the year 963. It was the remoteness from the distractions of city life and its problems that was the reason for many Byzantine monks over the centuries 'leaving the world' and joining one of the monasteries on the Holy Mountain.

heir to St John Chrysostom, still lives in Istanbul, but the patriarchate has a beleaguered quality about it; the compound is surrounded by a massive wall and heavy doors. Its church, rebuilt in the eighteenth century in such a way that its dome is concealed, in order that the eyes of fanatical Muslims passing by should not have to endure it, houses only a very few of the relics held before the conquest. A combination of destruction, oppression and neglect has eliminated almost everything else of the city of Constantine and Justinian.

It is the non-physical aspects of Byzantine civilization which are most enduring. The respect for and love of learning, the spiritual values and discipline which led to the creation of such profound forms of artistic expression, the intense pride in tradition — these are the qualities that seem so impressive to the modern, scientifically-oriented world. Just as Byzantium was, in its foundation, a civilization based on ideals, rather than on physical or ethnic unity, so it is Byzantium's ideals which have persisted vividly through the centuries to give inspiration today.

Below: This view of the battered, crumbling walls of Constantinople with the remains of a Turkish cemetery outside, contains in microcosm the history of the two major epochs in the city's life — its early centuries as the walled capital of a major empire, and its later life as the centre of the greatest Islamic power in the world.

Right: Fourteenth-century mosaic in a niche behind a pierced marble screen. St Mark's, Venice. The skull, symbol of death, is seen against a vine, suggesting judgement and redemption.

CHRONOLOGY:

THE BYZANTINE EMPERORS AND THEIR DYNASTIES

Dynasty of Constantine

Constantine I, The Great	330-337
Constantius	337-361
Julian, The Apostate	361-363
Jovian	363-364
Valens	364-378

Dynasty of Theodosius

Theodosius I, The Great	379-395
Arcadius	395-408
Theodosius II	408-450
Marcian	450-457

Dynasty of Leo

Leo I	457-474
Leo II	474
Zeno	474-491
Anastasius I	491-518

Dynasty of Justinian

Justin I	518-527
Justinian I	527-565
Justin II	565-578
Tiberius II	578-582
Maurice	582-602
Phocas	602-610

Dynasty of Heraclius

Heraclius I	610-641
Constantine III	641
Constans II	641-668
Constantine IV, Pogonatus	668-685
Justinian II, Rhinotmetus	685-695
	and 705-711

Leontius	695-698
Tiberius III	698-705

Non-dynastic

Philippicus Barbanes	711-713
Anastasius II	713-716
Theodosius III	716-717

Isaurian Dynasty

Leo III, The Isaurian	717-740
Constantine V, Copronymus	740-775
Leo IV	775-780
Constantine VI	780-797
Irene	797-802

Non-dynastic

Nicephorus I	802-811
Stauracius	811
Michael I, Rhangabe	811-813
Leo V	813-820

Amorian Dynasty

Michael II, The Stammerer	820-829
Theophilus	829-842
Michael III, The Drunkard	842-867

Macedonian Dynasty

Basil I	867-886
Leo VI, The Wise	886-912
Alexander	886 (912) -913
Constantine VII Porphyrogenitus	913-959
Romanus II	959-963

Non-dynastic usurpers:

Nicephorus II Phocas	**963-969**
John I Tzimisces	**969-976**

Macedonian Dynasty

Basil II Bulgaroctonus	**976-1025**
Constantine VIII	**1025-1028**
Romanus III, Argyrus	**1028-1034**
Michael IV, The Paphlagonian	**1034-1041**
Michael V	**1041-1042**
Zoe and Theodora	**1042**
Constantine IX Monomachus	**1042-1055**
Theodora	**1055-1056**

Non-dynastic:

Michael VI Stratioticus	**1056-1057**

Dynasty of the Dukas and Comnenes

Isaac I Comnenus	**1057-1059**
Constantine X Dukas	**1059-1067**
Michael VII	**1067-1068**
Nicephorus III Botaniates	**1078-1081**

Dynasty of the Comnenes

Alexius I Comnenus	**1081-1118**
John II	**1118-1143**
Manuel I	**1143-1180**
Alexius II	**1180-1183**
Andronicus I	**1183-1185**

Dynasty of the Angeli

Isaac II Angelus	**1185-1195**
Alexius III	**1195-1203**

Alexius IV	**1203-1204**

The Western Emperors of Constantinople

Baldwin of Flanders	**1204-1205**
Henry of Flanders	**1206-1216**
Peter of Courtenay	**1217**
Yolande	**1217-1219**
Robert II of Courtenay	**1221-1228**
Baldwin II	**1228-1261**

The Greek Emperors of Nicaea
Dynasty of the Lascarids

Theodore I Lascaris	**1204-1222**
John III Dukas Tatatzes	**1222-1254**
Theodore II Lascaris Vatatzes	**1254-1258**
John IV Dukas Tatatzes	**1258**

Usurper:

Michael VIII Palaeologus	**1258-1261**

Dynasty of the Palaeologues

Michael VIII Palaeologus	**1261-1282**
Andronicus II	**1282-1328**
Andronicus III	**1328-1341**
John V	**1341-1376**

Usurper:

John VI Cantacuzenus	**1347-1355**
Andronicus IV	**1376-1379**
John V	**1379-1390**
Manuel II	**1391-1425**
John VIII	**1425-1448**
Constantine XI Dragases	**1448-1453**

NOTE ON QUOTATIONS USED IN THE TEXT

Except where otherwise specifically indicated, all quotations have been translated from their original language by the author; the editions used have been standard ones, such as those of the Bonn *Corpus scriptorum historiae Byzantinae*. The only exception to this is the account by Ruy de Clavijo of his embassy to Tamerlane, quotations from which have been based on the translation published by Routledge in 1928, but with reference to the original Spanish edition.

ACKNOWLEDGEMENTS

Werner Forman and the publishers would like to acknowledge the help of the following museums and private collections in permitting the photography shown on the pages listed:
The Barber Institute of Fine Arts, the University of Birmingham: 13, 30, 36, 72, 74 below, 76 above and below; Biblioteca Nacional, Madrid: 28 below, 33 below, 65, 66 above and below, 67, 68 above and below, 69 above and below; Biblioteca Nazionale Marciana, Venice: 31, 46, 71, 79 below, 116; British Museum, London: 8, 9 above, 41 below, 54, 60 above and below, 77 above and below, 78 left and right, 80 top, 81 above and below, 84, 85; Byzantine Museum, Athens: 32, 33 above, 41 above, 42, 43, 44, 45, 55 above and below, 83 above, 88, 89, 91; Cathedral Treasury, Limburg: 101, 102, 103, 104, 105; Erzbischöslichen Diözesan-museum, Cologne: 82; Früh-christlich-Byzantinche Sammlung, Berlin: 11, 106 below; Istanbul Arkeoloji Müzeleri, Istanbul: 83 below; Metropolitan Museum, New York, 1 [Byzantine gold cup — gift of J. Pierpont Morgan, 1917]; Mosaics Museum, Istanbul: 6, 92; National Library, Athens: 3, 7, 40, 63, 94 all, 95 96 above and below, 97, 99, 100 above, 112 right; Real Academia de la Historia, Madrid: 4, 62; Thessaloniki Archeological Museum: 80 middle; Topkapi Palace Library, Istanbul: 119; Topkapi Palace Museum, Istanbul: 48, 49 above; Treasury of the Basilica of the Virgin, Maastricht; 86, 87; Treasury of St Mark's, Venice: 112 left, 113.

Werner Forman would also like to thank the following for their assistance:
Nata Bàzas, Athens; Ms. Emine Bilirgen, Istanbul; David Buckton, London; Ms. R. Callegari, Venice; Marian Campbell, London; Catherine Cordouli, Athens; Prof. Victor Elbern, Berlin; Afif Süreyya Duruçay, Istanbul; Margaret Frazer, New York; Nubar Hampartumian, Birmingham; Cengiz Köseoglü, Istanbul; Dr. D. Kötzsche, Berlin; Pavlos Lazaridis, Athens; Manuel Sanchez Mariana, Madrid; B. Matthai, Cologne; Prof. H. A. D. Miles, Birmingham; P. G. Nikolopoulos, Athens; J. Pick, Limburg; Katerina Romiopoulou, Thessaloniki; Dr. W. Schulten, Cologne; Hipolito Escolar Sobrino, Madrid; Dr. J. Sprenger, Limburg; Mrs. Zeren Tanindi, Istanbul; Mrs. Aysel Tuzenlar, Istanbul; Julia Vokotopoulou, Thessaloniki.

BIBLIOGRAPHY

Baynes, N. H. and Moss, H. St. L. B. *Byzantium: An Introduction to Byzantine Civilisation*. Oxford 1961.

Beckwith, J. *The Art of Constantinople: An Introduction to Byzantine Art*. London 1968. *Early Christian and Byzantine Art*. Harmondsworth 1970.

Demus, O. *Byzantine Mosaic Decoration*. London 1953; New Rochelle, N. Y. 1976.

Haussig, H. W. *A History of Byzantine Civilisation*. London 1971; Atlantic Highlands, N. J. 1971.

Hearsey, J. E. N. *City of Constantine*. London 1963.

Krautheimer, R. *Early Christian and Byzantine Architecture*. Harmondsworth 1975.

Mango, C. *The Art of the Byzantine Empire 312—1453: Sources and Documents in the History of Art*. Englewood Cliffs, N. J. 1972.

Mathew, G. *Byzantine Aesthetics* London 1963.

Mathews, T. F. *The Early Churches of Constantinople: Architecture and Liturgy*. University Park, Pennsylvania 1972.

Runciman, S. *Byzantine Civilisation*. London 1933, 1961; New York 1933. *The Fall of Constantinople, 1453*. Cambridge 1969. *The Great Church in Captivity: Study of the Patriarchate of Constantinople from the Eve of the Turkish Conquest to the Greek War of Independence*. Cambridge 1968.

Tanner, J. R. *et al.*, ed. *The Cambridge Medieval History*, vol. 4, parts 1 and 2. Cambridge 1966 and 1967.

Underwood, P., ed. *The Kariye Djami*, 4 vols. London 1967—73; Princeton, N. J. 1975.

Vasiliev, A. A. *History of the Byzantine Empire*, 2 vols. Magnolia, Minnesota 1958.

Wilson, N. G. *et al. Byzantine Books and Bookmen*. Washington, D. C. 1975.

INDEX